SLAVERY IN AMERICAN SOCIETY

PROBLEMS IN AMERICAN CIVILIZATION

SLAVERY IN AMERICAN SOCIETY

EDITED WITH AN INTRODUCTION BY

Richard D. Brown

OBERLIN COLLEGE

D. C. HEATH AND COMPANY
Lexington, Massachusetts

Library of Congress Catalog Card Number: 70–88757

CONTENTS

INTRODUCTION

SLAVERY and its distinctive pattern of race relations have long exercised a decisive role in shaping American society. Although a full century separates us from slavery as an established institution, its heritage remains a dynamic force of immense proportions. Our own attitudes, patterns of behavior, and institutions continue to reflect impulses which were generated in a system which has long since vanished. As a result this defunct social institution retains a profound continuity with our own times, possessing a special immediacy for contemporary society.

No one planned the creation of American Negro slavery. Like many American novelties it was a synthesis produced by interaction between the colonists and their environment. Ironically, the Englishmen who created slavery and who were responsible for modeling most colonial institutions came from a nation which boasted that it knew no law of slavery, and that English soil was synonymous with personal and political freedom. Nevertheless, social arrangements resembling a racial caste system emerged as a central feature of Anglo-American society.

The first challenge to English social conceptions came from the Indians. Here, after some small efforts at assimilation, English colonists responded to the problems of ethnic heterogeneity by displacing or destroying the natives, ultimately rejecting them as alien enemies. This solution seemed to permit the development of a purely European Christian society. But the racial homogeneity of European society in North America was never actually established. At the same time that Indians disappeared from English settlements, Africans entered. Their entry—first in small numbers, later by the thousand—produced a variety of social and religious challenges to the societies of the scattered English settlements. Yet their solutions were remarkably uniform: everywhere they established the supremacy of Europeans and the subjection of Africans.

Supremacy, by the early eighteenth century, meant that chattel slavery was the normal status of African immigrants in every colony. As chattels, Africans became articles of moveable property devoid of the minimum human rights recognized by society. Unless they could show written proof of free status, hereditary lifelong servitude had become the fixed condition of any colonist with at least one African parent or grandparent. A servant caste was emerging, intimately connected with many phases of colonial social life, yet regarded with disdain and excluded from sharing the social and economic mobility which was an essential condition of white men in the developing society. Negroes lived in the dynamic, competitive, exploitative society not as willing actors but largely as manipulated, often hostile, servants —in but not of American society.

This pattern of white supremacy and black subjection has been so much a part of American life that it was long seen as inevitable. Until the Second World War most historians believed that given the intensive colonial demand for labor, the physical and ethnic characteristics of the two races necessarily established white men as masters over black slaves. But since 1945 a new, consciously anti-racist attitude has characterized inquiry into the development of American race relations. Now, the particular pattern of white subjection of blacks—however natural and necessary it may have seemed to generations of Americans— demands explanation. Historians wonder why Englishmen invented a new slave status in their midst, and why they attached it to Africans. Moreover they wonder why slavery in Anglo and Latin America produced such radically different patterns of race relations. In the last generation they have begun to answer these questions by examining the process whereby captive Africans were transformed into the classic, ante-bellum American Negro chattel slave.

In Anglo-America the events of the seventeenth century were crucial. Winthrop Jordan's analysis, comparing the development of slavery in New England with its growth in both the Chesapeake Bay region and the British West Indies, reveals how a variety of forces converged to establish the institution firmly by 1700. Once created, North American slavery was a dynamic social force. As the studies of Tate, Klein, Litwack, and Stampp demonstrate, both the character of slavery and race relations experienced continuous mutation throughout the ante-bellum period. In the North this included the peaceful abolition of slavery, while in the South, eighteenth- and nineteenth-century developments intensified the special character of American slavery and its impact on society.

This "special" character of American race relations stands out when slavery in Anglo-America is compared with its Latin American counterpart. There, it has been argued, the humanity of slaves was recognized and Negroes were not reduced to the subhuman status of chattels. Frank Tannenbaum explains these differences in terms of religion and tradition. He starts from the premise that the "humane" Roman legal and customary traditions of multi-racial slavery had been preserved in the Iberian peninsula until the era of American settlement. Therefore when Spanish and Portuguese conquistadors established slavery in the New World, it was tempered by these traditions which were reinforced by the activities of the Catholic Church, a powerful institution whose concern for the salvation of souls embraced all races. By contrast, since the English lacked a slave tradition as well as a strong colonial ecclesiastical establishment, they fitted slavery into their law of property. As a result Tannenbaum believes that North American Negroes, who were not protected by a universal church, came to be regarded as objects.

Tannenbaum's argument has long exercised wide influence on interpreters of slavery and race. But recently it has been challenged frontally by Marvin Harris, an anthropologist; Harmannus Hoetink, a sociologist; and David Brion Davis, an historian. Harris agrees that race relations differed radically in North and South America, but he attributes the explanation to objective demographic and socio-economic circumstances rather than broad cultural factors like secular and religious traditions. Moreover he finds that the specific patterns of race relations in the Americas were functional for their societies; thus for him the historical dimension becomes virtually irrelevant. Present, not past, circumstances dictated the basic structure of social relations.

Hoetink's criticism of Tannenbaum, while in some ways similar to Harris's, emphasizes the influence of economic factors which Tannenbaum ignored. Hoetink further points out that the conventional North American racial categories of "Negro" and "white" employed by Tannenbaum are inapplicable to Brazilian society. They obscure the operation of a racial prejudice common to both societies. In Hoetink's view, Latin and Anglo-American slavery and race relations are simply variant forms of a single pattern common to the entire Caribbean basin.

The historian David Davis treats Tannenbaum more sympathetically, since he too regards cultural and historical forces as vital in explaining social behavior. But his observations differ, and they lead to conclusions parallel with Hoetink's. For unlike Tannenbaum, Davis refuses to accept formal legal codes as descriptive of the practice of slavery in either North or South America. Instead he finds ample testimony showing that whatever laws were on the books, slave personality received as little recognition on Latin American plantations as it did in Anglo-America. Davis goes on to stress the common characteristics of slavery in the Americas, concluding that while slaves nowhere enjoyed full recognition of their humanity, they were nowhere reduced absolutely to chattel status. As a result he has implicitly challenged the meaning of such common analytic concepts as "slavery" and "chattel," demanding more sophisticated interpretation.

Another consequence of Davis's work is his demonstration that scholars tend to work from within accepted, conventional interpretations, without challenging the standard conceptualization of a problem. The same tendency may be observed regarding slavery and race in American social life. Here they have been regarded as Southern rather than American topics, and so relatively little attention has been directed toward their impact on the whole society. Today, however, the prominence of national race problems has undercut the relevance of the old sectional conceptualization. Nevertheless, certain recent analyses of slavery in the context of Southern society may have a broader applicability, illuminating the nature of race relations generally. Leaning heavily on Tannenbaum's work, Stanley Elkins argues that chattel slavery was a consequence of capitalism applied to agriculture, and that race relations took their character from the positions of the white and the black in a capitalist culture. Eugene Genovese replies by arguing that Southern society was more paternal and anti-bourgeois than it was capitalist, and that race relations, like the economy, followed patterns common to traditional societies. Taken together, the two arguments imply that the evolution of slavery and race relations are inseparable from the general character of American society.

Slavery should not, therefore, be examined in isolation. Throughout its history the institution and its internal characteristics were always enmeshed in larger patterns of social life. The traditional conception of America as a free society has put slavery and its patterns of behavior conveniently outside the mainstream, making them anomalies to be dealt with as special cases, since slavery did not become the general pattern of American life and was extinguished in 1865. But if patterns of behavior between whites and blacks, as between other ethnic groups, are part of the mainstream of American history, then slavery must be included. Examination of the origins and evolution of American Negro slavery becomes necessary for an understanding of American society, while a comparative approach adds a dimension of conceptual leverage frequently absent from historical analysis.

CONFLICT OF OPINION

Scholars disagree in their explanations of the social character of slavery:

> Under the influence of law and religion, the social milieu in the Spanish and Portuguese colonies made easy room for the Negroes passing from slavery to freedom.
>
> —FRANK TANNENBAUM

> If past laws and values had a significant role to play in the treatment of Negroes and mulattoes, the hounding persecution of the free Negroes and mulattoes should never have occurred in the English colonies.
>
> —MARVIN HARRIS

> If an exploitive, capitalistic form of servitude was at times common in Brazil and Spanish America, and if North Americans conformed at times to a paternalistic model and openly acknowledged the humanity of their slaves, it may be that differences between slavery in Latin America and the United States were no greater than regional or temporal differences within the countries themselves.
>
> —DAVID B. DAVIS

Moreover there is controversy as to whether slavery took its character from dominant social values, or whether in fact it determined them:

> With the full development of the plantation there was nothing . . . to prevent unmitigated capitalism from becoming unmitigated slavery. The planter was now engaged in capitalistic agriculture with a labor force entirely under his control. . . . It was in such a setting that those rights of personality traditionally regarded between men as private and inherent, quite apart from the matter of lifetime servitude, were left virtually without defense.
>
> —STANLEY M. ELKINS

> The planters were not mere capitalists; they were pre-capitalist, quasi-aristocratic landowners. . . . Their society, in its spirit and fundamental direction, represented the antithesis of capitalism, however many compromises it had to make.
>
> —EUGENE D. GENOVESE

I. THE EMERGENCE OF SLAVERY IN ANGLO-AMERICA

Winthrop D. Jordan

UNTHINKING DECISION: ENSLAVEMENT OF NEGROES IN AMERICA TO 1700

In the following essay Professor Jordan provides a comparative analysis of the emergence of chattel slavery in the English mainland colonies. His study, revealing the interaction between social attitudes and social institutions, is the most nearly definitive treatment of the origin of slavery in Anglo-America available. It represents the culmination of a debate among scholars which has stretched over a full generation. The selection is drawn from Jordan's landmark study of early American race relations, *White Over Black: American Attitudes Toward the Negro, 1550–1812.* Professor Jordan teaches at the University of California, Berkeley.

AT the start of English settlement in America, no one had in mind to establish the institution of Negro slavery. Yet in less than a century the foundations of a peculiar institution had been laid. The first Negroes landed in Virginia in 1619, though very, very little is known about their precise status during the next twenty years. Between 1640 and 1660 there is evidence of enslavement, and after 1660 slavery crystallized on the statute books of Maryland, Virginia, and other colonies. By 1700 when African Negroes began flooding into English America they were treated as somehow deserving a life and status radically different from English and other European settlers. The Negro had been debased to a condition of chattel slavery; at some point, Englishmen in America had created a legal status which ran counter to English law.

Unfortunately the details of this proc-ess can never be completely reconstructed; there is simply not enough evidence (and very little chance of more to come) to show precisely when and how and why Negroes came to be treated so differently from white men, though there is just enough to make historians differ as to its meaning. Concerning the first years of contact especially we have very little information as to what impression Negroes made upon English settlers: accordingly, we are left knowing less about the formative years than about later periods of American slavery. That those early years were crucial ones is obvious, for it was then that the cycle of Negro debasement began; once the Negro became fully the slave it is not hard to see why white men looked down upon him. Yet precisely because understanding the dynamics of these early years is so important to understanding the centuries which followed, it is neces-

From Winthrop D. Jordan, *White Over Black* (Chapel Hill: University of North Carolina Press, 1968) pp. 44–98. Reprinted by permission of the University of North Carolina Press and the Institute of Early American History and Culture. Documenting footnotes in this and several of the subsequent selections have been omitted.

sary to bear with the less than satisfactory data and to attempt to reconstruct the course of debasement undergone by Negroes in seventeenth-century America. In order to comprehend it, we need first of all to examine certain social pressures generated by the American environment and how these pressures interacted with certain qualities of English social thought and law that existed on the eve of settlement, qualities that even then were being modified by examples set by England's rivals for empire in the New World.

THE NECESSITIES OF A NEW WORLD

When Englishmen crossed the Atlantic to settle in America, they were immediately subject to novel strains. In some settlements, notably Jamestown and Plymouth, the survival of the community was in question. An appalling proportion of people were dead within a year, from malnutrition, starvation, unconquerable diseases, bitter cold, oppressive heat, Indian attacks, murder, and suicide. The survivors were isolated from the world as they had known it, cut off from friends and family and the familiar sights and sounds and smells which have always told men who and where they are. A similar sense of isolation and disorientation was inevitable even in the settlements that did not suffer through a starving time. English settlers were surrounded by savages. They had to perform a round of daily tasks to which most were unaccustomed. They had undergone the shock of detachment from home in order to set forth upon a dangerous voyage of from ten to thirteen weeks that ranged from unpleasant to fatal and that seared into every passenger's memory the ceaselessly tossing distance that separated him from his old way of life.

Life in America put great pressure upon the traditional social and economic controls that Englishmen assumed were to be exercised by civil and often ecclesiastical authority. Somehow the empty woods seemed to lead much more toward license than restraint. At the same time, by reaction, this unfettering resulted in an almost pathetic so-

cial conservatism, a yearning for the forms and symbols of the old familiar social order. . . . English social forms were transplanted to America not simply because they were nice to have around but because without them the new settlements would have fallen apart and English settlers would have become men of the forest, savage men devoid of civilization.

For the same reason, the communal goals that animated the settlement of the colonies acquired great functional importance in the wilderness; they served as antidotes to social and individual disintegration. The physical hardships of settlement could never have been surmounted without the stiffened nerve and will engendered by commonly recognized if sometimes unarticulated purposes. In New England lack of articulation was no problem. The Puritans knew precisely who they were (the chosen of God, many of them) and that they were seeking to erect a Godly community. Though that community (eventually) eluded them, they retained their conviction that they manned a significant outpost of English civilization. As Cotton Mather grandly told the Massachusetts governor and General Court in 1700, "It is no Little Blessing of God, that we are a part of the *English nation*." A similar deep sense of self-transplantation buttressed the settlements in Virginia and Maryland. While there was less talk than in New England about God's special endorsement, virtually every settler knew that Englishmen were serving His greater glory by removing to Virginia and by making a prosperous success of the project. They recognized also that their efforts at western planting aggrandized English wealth and power and the cause of reformed Christianity. . . . For Englishmen planting in America, then, it was of the utmost importance to know that they were Englishmen, which was to say that they were educated (to a degree suitable to their station), Christian (of an appropriate Protestant variety), civilized, and (again to an appropriate degree) free men.

It was with personal freedom, of

course, that wilderness conditions most suddenly reshaped English laws, assumptions, and practices. In America land was plentiful, labor scarce, and, as in all new colonies, a cash crop desperately needed. These economic conditions were to remain important for centuries; in general they tended to encourage greater geographical mobility, less specialization, higher rewards, and fewer restraints on the processes and products of labor. Supporting traditional assumptions and practices, however, was the need to retain them simply because they were familiar and because they served the vital function of maintaining and advancing orderly settlement. Throughout the seventeenth century there were pressures on traditional practices which similarly told in opposite directions.

In general men who invested capital in agriculture in America came under fewer customary and legal restraints than in England concerning what they did with their land and with the people who worked on it. On the other hand their activities were constrained by the economic necessity of producing cash crops for export, which narrowed their choice of how they could treat it. Men without capital could obtain land relatively easily: hence the shortage of labor and the notably blurred line between men who had capital and men who did not. Men and women in England faced a different situation. A significant amount of capital was required in order to get to America, and the greatest barrier to material advancement in America was the Atlantic Ocean.

Three major systems of labor emerged amid the interplay of these social and economic conditions in America. One, which was present from the beginning, was free wage labor, in which contractual arrangements rested upon a monetary nexus. Another, which was the last to appear, was chattel slavery, in which there were no contractual arrangements (except among owners). The third, which virtually coincided with first settlement in America, was temporary servitude, in which complex contractual arrangements gave shape to the entire system. It was this third system, inden-

tured servitude, which permitted so many English settlers to cross the Atlantic barrier. Indentured servitude was linked to the development of chattel slavery in America, and its operation deserves closer examination.

A very sizable proportion of settlers in the English colonies came as indentured servants bound by contract to serve a master for a specified number of years, usually from four to seven or until age twenty-one, as repayment for their ocean passage. The time of service to which the servant bound himself was negotiable property, and he might be sold or conveyed from one master to another at any time up to the expiration of his indenture, at which point he became a free man. (Actually it was his *labor* which was owned and sold, not his *person*, though this distinction was neither important nor obvious at the time.) Custom and statute law regulated the relationship between servant and master. Obligation was reciprocal: the master undertook to feed and clothe and sometimes to educate his servant and to refrain from abusing him, while the servant was obliged to perform such work as his master set him and to obey his master in all things. This typical pattern, with a multitude of variations, was firmly established by mid-seventeenth century. In Virginia and Maryland, both the legal and actual conditions of servants seem to have improved considerably from the early years when servants had often been outrageously abused and sometimes forced to serve long terms. Beginning about 1640 the legislative assemblies of the two colonies passed numerous acts prescribing maximum terms of service and requiring masters to pay the customary "freedom dues" (clothing, provisions, and so forth) at the end of the servant's time. This legislation may have been actuated partly by the need to attract more immigrants with guarantees of good treatment, in which case underpopulation in relation to level of technology and to natural resources in the English colonies may be said to have made for greater personal freedom. On the other hand, it may also have been a matter of protecting traditional freedoms threatened by this same fact of underpopulation which generated so powerful a need for labor which would not be transient and temporary. In this instance, very clearly, the imperatives enjoined by settlement in the wilderness interacted with previously acquired ideas concerning personal freedom. Indeed without some inquiry into Elizabethan thinking on that subject, it will remain impossible to comprehend why Englishmen became servants in the plantations, and Negroes slaves.

FREEDOM AND BONDAGE
IN THE ENGLISH TRADITION

Thinking about freedom and bondage in Tudor England was confused and self-contradictory. In a period of social dislocation there was considerable disagreement among contemporary observers as to what actually was going on and even as to what ought to be. Ideas about personal freedom tended to run both ahead of and behind actual social conditions. Both statute and common law were sometimes considerably more than a century out of phase with actual practice and with commonly held notions about servitude. Finally, ideas and practices were changing rapidly. It is possible, however, to identify certain important tenets of social thought that served as anchor points amid this chaos.

Englishmen lacked accurate methods of ascertaining what actually was happening to their social institutions, but they were not wrong in supposing that villenage, or "bondage" as they more often called it, had virtually disappeared in England. William Harrison put the matter most strenuously in 1577: "As for slaves and bondmen we have none, naie such is the privilege of our countrie by the especiall grace of God, and bountie of our princes, that if anie come hither from other realms, so soone as they set foot on land they become so free of condition as their masters, whereby all note of servile bondage is utterlie remooved from them." Other observers were of the (correct) opinion that a few lingering vestiges—bondmen whom the progress of freedom had passed by— might still be found in the crannies of

the decayed manorial system, but everyone agreed that such vestiges were anachronistic. In fact there were English men and women who were still "bond" in the mid-sixteenth century, but they were few in number and their status was much more a technicality than a condition. In the middle ages, being a villein had meant dependence upon the will of a feudal lord but by no means deprivation of all social and legal rights. In the thirteenth and fourteenth centuries villenage had decayed markedly, and it may be said not to have existed as a viable social institution in the second half of the sixteenth century. Personal freedom had become the normal status of Englishmen. Most contemporaries welcomed this fact; indeed it was after about 1550 that there began to develop in England that preening consciousness of the peculiar glories of English liberties.

How had it all happened? Among those observers who tried to explain, there was agreement that Christianity was primarily responsible. They thought of villenage as a mitigation of ancient bond slavery and that the continuing trend to liberty was animated, as Sir Thomas Smith said in a famous passage, by the "perswasion . . . of Christians not to make nor keepe his brother in Christ, servile, bond and underling for ever unto him, as a beast rather than as a man." They agreed also that the trend had been forwarded by the common law, in which the disposition was always, as the phrase went, *in favorem libertatis*, "in favor of liberty." Probably they were correct in both these suppositions, but the common law harbored certain inconsistencies as to freedom which may have had an important though imponderable effect upon the reappearance of slavery in English communities in the seventeenth century.

The accreted structure of the common law sometimes resulted in imperviousness to changing conditions. The first book of Lord Coke's great *Institutes of the Laws of England* (1628), for example, was an extended gloss upon Littleton's fifteenth-century treatise on *Tenures* and it repeatedly quoted the opinions of such famous authorities as Bracton, who had died in 1268. When Bracton had described villenage, English law had not yet fully diverged from the civil or Roman law, and villenage actually existed. Almost four hundred years later some legal authorities were still citing Bracton on villenage without even alluding to the fact that villenage no longer existed. . . . Thus while villenage was actually extinct, it lay unmistakably fossilized in the common law. Its survival in that rigid form must have reminded Englishmen that there existed a sharply differing alternative to personal liberty. It was in this vague way that villenage seems to have been related to the development of chattel slavery in America. Certainly villenage was not the forerunner of slavery, but its survival in the law books meant that a possibility which might have been foreclosed was not. Later, after Negro slavery had clearly emerged, English lawyers were inclined to think of slavery as being a New World version of the ancient tenure described by Bracton and Cowell and Coke.

That the common law was running centuries behind social practice was only one of several important factors complicating Tudor thought about the proper status of individuals in society. The social ferment of the sixteenth century resulted not only in the impalpable mood of control and subordination which seems to have affected English perception of Africans but also in the well-known strenuous efforts of Tudor governments to lay restrictions on elements in English society which seemed badly out of control. From at least the 1530's the countryside swarmed with vagrants, sturdy beggars, rogues, and vagabonds, with men who could but would not work. They committed all manner of crimes, the worst of which was remaining idle. It was an article of faith among Tudor commentators (before there were "Puritans" to help propound it) that idleness was the mother of all vice and the chief danger to a well-ordered state. Tudor statesmen valiantly attempted to suppress idleness by means of the famous vagrancy laws which provided for houses of correction and (finally) for whipping the vagrant from constable to constable until he reached his home parish. They assumed that everyone belonged in a specific social niche and that anyone failing to labor in the niche assigned to him by Providence must be compelled to do so by authority.

Some experiments in compulsion ran counter to the trend toward personal liberty. In 1547, shortly after the death of Henry VIII, a parliamentary statute provided that any able-bodied person adjudged a vagabond upon presentment to two justices of the peace should be branded with a "V" on the chest and made a "slave" for two years to the presenter who was urged to give "the saide Slave breade and water or small dryncke and such refuse of meate as he shall thincke mete [and] cause the said Slave to worke by beating cheyninge or otherwise in such worke and Labor how vyle so ever it be." Masters could "putt a rynge of Iron about his Necke Arme or his Legge for a more knowledge and suretie of the keepinge of him." A runaway "slave" convicted by a court was to be branded on the cheek or forehead and adjudged "to be the saide Masters Slave for ever." These provisions reflected desperation. Fully as significant as their passage was their repeal three years later by a statute which frankly asserted in the preamble that their "extremitie" had "byn occation that they have not ben putt in ure [use]."

Englishmen generally were unwilling to submit or subscribe to such debasement. Despite a brief statutory experiment with banishment "beyond the Seas" and with judgment "perpetually to the Gallyes of this Realme" in 1598, Tudor authorities gradually hammered out the legal framework of a labor system which permitted compulsion but which did not permit so total a loss of freedom as lifetime hereditary slavery. Apprenticeship seemed to them the ideal status, for apprenticeship provided a means of regulating the economy and of guiding youth into acceptable paths of honest industry. By 1600, many writers had come to think of other kinds of bound labor as inferior forms of apprentice-

ship, involving less of an educative function, less permanence, and a less rigidly
contractual basis. This tendency to reason from apprenticeship downward,
rather than from penal service up, had
the important effect of imparting some
of the very strong contractualism in the
master-apprentice relationship to less
formal varieties of servitude. There were
"indentured" servants in England prior
to English settlement in America. Their
written "indentures" gave visible evidence of the strong element of mutual
obligation between master and servant:
each retained a copy of the contract
which was "indented" at the top so as to
match the other.

As things turned out, it was indentured servitude which best met the requirements for settling in America. Of
course there were other forms of bound
labor which contributed to the process
of settlement: many convicts were sent
and many children abducted. Yet among
all the numerous varieties and degrees
of non-freedom which existed in England, there was none which could have
served as a well-formed model for the
chattel slavery which developed in
America. This is not to say, though, that
slavery was an unheard-of novelty in
Tudor England. On the contrary, "bond
slavery" was a memory trace of long
standing. Vague and confused as the
concept of slavery was in the minds of
Englishmen, it possessed certain fairly
consistent connotations which were to
help shape English perceptions of the
way Europeans should properly treat the
newly discovered peoples overseas.

THE CONCEPT OF SLAVERY

At first glance, one is likely to see
merely a fog of inconsistency and vagueness enveloping the terms *servant* and
slave as they were used both in England
and in seventeenth-century America.
When Hamlet declaims "O what a rogue
and peasant slave am I," the term seems
to have a certain elasticity. When Peter
Heylyn defines it in 1627 as "that igno-
minious word, *Slave;* whereby we use to
call ignoble fellowes, and the more base
sort of people," the term seems useless

as a key to a specific social status. And
when we find in the American colonies
a reference in 1665 to "Jacob a negro
slave and servant to Nathaniel Utye," it
is tempting to regard slavery as having
been in the first half of the seventeenth
century merely a not very elevated sort
of servitude.

In one sense it was, since the concept
embodied in the terms *servitude, service,* and *servant* was widely embracive.
Servant was more a generic term than
slave. Slaves could be "servants"—as
they were eventually and ironically to
become in the ante-bellum South—but
servants *should not* be "slaves." This in-
junction, which was common in England, suggests a measure of precision in
the concept of slavery. In fact there was
a large measure which merits closer in-
spection.

First of all, the "slave's" loss of freedom was complete. "Of all men which
be destitute of libertie or freedome," explained Henry Swinburne in his *Briefe
Treatise of Testaments and Last Willes*
(1590), "the slave is in greatest subjection, for a slave is that person which is
in servitude or bondage to an other, even
against nature." "Even his children,"
moreover, ". . . are infected with the Lep-
rosie of his father's bondage." Swinburne was at pains to distinguish this
condition from that of the villein, whom
he likened to the *Ascriptitius Glebæ* of
the civil law, "one that is ascrited or assigned to a ground or farme, for the perpetuall tilling or manuring thereof." "A
villeine," he insisted, "howsoever he may
seeme like unto a slave, yet his bondage
is not so great." Swinburne's was the
prevailing view of bond slavery; only the
preciseness of emphasis was unusual.
At law, much more clearly than in liter-
ary usage, "bond slavery" implied utter
deprivation of liberty.

Slavery was also thought of as a perpetual condition. While it had not yet
come invariably to mean lifetime labor,
it was frequently thought of in those
terms. Except sometimes in instances of
punishment for crime, slavery was open
ended; in contrast to servitude, it did not
involve a definite term of years. Slavery

was perpetual also in the sense that it was often thought of as hereditary. It was these dual aspects of perpetuity which were to assume such importance in America.

So much was slavery a complete loss of liberty that it seemed to Englishmen somehow akin to loss of humanity. No theme was more persistent than the claim that to treat a man as a slave was to treat him as a beast. Almost half a century after Sir Thomas Smith had made this connection a Puritan divine was condemning masters who used "their servants as slaves, or rather as beasts" while Captain John Smith was moaning about being captured by the Turks and "all sold for slaves, like beasts in a market-place." No analogy could have better demonstrated how strongly Englishmen felt about total loss of personal freedom.

Certain prevalent assumptions about the origins of slavery paralleled this analogy at a different level of intellectual construction. Lawyers and divines alike assumed that slavery was impossible before the Fall, that it violated natural law, that it was instituted by positive human laws, and, more generally, that in various ways it was connected with sin. These ideas were as old as the church fathers and the Roman writers on natural law. In the social atmosphere of pre-Restoration England it was virtually inevitable that they should have been capsulated in the story of Ham. . . . Sir Edward Coke (himself scarcely a Puritan) declared, "This is assured, That Bondage or Servitude was first inflicted for dishonouring of Parents: For Cham the Father of Canaan . . . seeing the Nakedness of his Father Noah, and shewing it in Derision to his Brethren, was therefore punished in his Son Canaan with Bondage."

The great jurist wrote this in earnest, but at least he did offer another description of slavery's genesis. In it he established what was perhaps the most important and widely acknowledged attribute of slavery: at the time of the Flood "all Things were common to all," but afterward, with the emergence of private property, there "arose battles"; "then it was ordained by Constitution of Nations . . . that he that was taken in Battle should remain Bond to his taker for ever, and he to do with him, all that should come of him, his Will and Pleasure, as with his Beast, or any other Cattle, to give, or to sell, or to kill." This final power, Coke noted, had since been taken away (owing to "the Cruelty of some Lords") and placed in the hands only of kings. The animating rationale here was that captivity in war meant an end to a person's claim to life as a human being; by sparing the captive's life, the captor acquired virtually absolute power over the life of the man who had lost the power to control his own.

More than any other single quality, *captivity* differentiated slavery from servitude. Although there were other, subsidiary ways of becoming a slave, such as being born of slave parents, selling oneself into slavery, or being adjudged to slavery for crime, none of these were considered to explain the way slavery had originated. Slavery was a power relationship; servitude was a relationship of service. Men were "slaves" to the devil but "servants" of God. Men were "galley-slaves," not galley servants. Bondage had never existed in the county of Kent because Kent was "never vanquished by [William] the Conquerour, but yeelded it selfe by composition."

This tendency to equate slavery with captivity had important ramifications. Warfare was usually waged against another people; captives were usually foreigners—"strangers" as they were termed. Until the emergence of nation-states in Europe, by far the most important category of strangers was the non-Christian. International warfare seemed above all a ceaseless struggle between Christians and Turks. Slavery, therefore, frequently appeared to rest upon the "perpetual enmity" which existed between Christians on the one hand and "infidels" and "pagans" on the other. In the sixteenth and seventeenth centuries Englishmen at home could read scores of accounts concerning the miserable fate of Englishmen and other Christians taken into "captivity" by Turks and Moors and oppressed by the "verie worst manner of bondmanship and slaverie." Clearly slavery was tinged by the religious disjunction.

Just as many commentators thought that the spirit of Christianity was responsible for the demise of bondage in England, many divines distinguished between ownership of Christian and of non-Christian servants. The Reverend William Gouge referred to "such servants as being strangers were bondslaves, over whom masters had a more absolute power than others." The Reverend Henry Smith declared, "He which counteth his servant a slave, is in error: for there is difference betweene beleeving servants and infidell servants." Implicit in every clerical discourse was the assumption that common brotherhood in Christ imparted a special quality to the master-servant relationship.

Slavery did not possess that quality, which made it fortunate that Englishmen did not enslave one another. As we have seen, however, Englishmen did possess a *concept* of slavery, formed by the clustering of several rough but not illogical equations. The slave was treated like a beast. Slavery was inseparable from the evil in men; it was God's punishment upon Ham's prurient disobedience. Enslavement was captivity, the loser's lot in a contest of power. Slaves were infidels or heathens.

On every count, Negroes qualified.

THE PRACTICES OF PORTINGALS AND SPANYARDS

Which is not to say that Englishmen were casting about for a people to enslave. What happened was that they found thrust before them not only instances of Negroes being taken into slavery but attractive opportunities for joining in that business. Englishmen actually were rather slow to seize these opportunities; on most of the sixteenth-century English voyages to West Africa there was no dealing in slaves. The notion that it was appropriate to do so seems to have been drawn chiefly from the example set by the Spanish and Portuguese.

Without inquiring into the reasons, it can be said that slavery had persisted since ancient times in the Iberian peninsula, that prior to the discoveries it was primarily a function of the religious wars against the Moors, that Portuguese explorers pressing down the coast in the fifteenth century captured thousands of Negroes whom they carried back to Portugal as slaves, and that after 1500, Portuguese ships began supplying the Spanish and Portuguese settlements in America with Negro slaves. By 1550 European enslavement of Negroes was more than a century old, and Negro slavery had become a fixture of the New World.

For present purposes there is no need to inquire into the precise nature of this slavery except to point out that in actual practice it did fit the English concept of bond slavery. The question which needs answering pertains to contemporary English knowledge of what was going on. And the answer may be given concisely: Englishmen had easily at hand a great deal of not very precise information. . . .

Some Englishmen decided that there might be profit in supplying the Spanish with Negroes, despite the somewhat theoretical prohibition of foreigners from the Spanish dominions in the New World. John Hawkins was first; in the 1560's he made three voyages to Africa, the islands, and home. The first two were very successful; the third met disaster at San Juan de Ulua when the Spanish attacked his ships, took most of them, and turned the captured English seamen over to the Inquisition. . . .

The Hawkins voyages were the principal but not the only instances where Englishmen had direct contact with the sixteenth-century trade in Negroes. . . . Long before English settlement in the New World, there were English merchants who knew the prices Negroes were bringing there. At the Admiralty Court hearing after the third Hawkins voyage, William Fowler, who had not been with Hawkins, was called in to testify concerning the value of the Negroes lost at San Juan de Ulua. Fowler deposed "that the best trade in those places is of Negroes: the trade whereof he hath used, and hath sold Negroes at the said places; and seen other merchants likewise sell their Negroes there, divers times."

By the end of the first quarter of the seventeenth century it had become abundantly evident in England that Negroes were being enslaved on an international scale. A century before, Leo Africanus had referred frequently to "Negro-slaves" in North Africa. By 1589 Negroes had become so pre-eminently "slaves" that Richard Hakluyt gratuitously referred to five Africans brought temporarily to England as "black slaves." Readers of Hakluyt, Purchas, and other popular accounts were informed that the Dutch had "Blacks (which are Slaves)" in the East Indies; that Greeks ventured "into Arabia to steale Negroes"; that the "blacks of Mozambique" were frequently taken as "slaves" to India, and, according to George Sandys, that near Cairo merchants purchased "Negroes" (for "slavery") who came from the upper Nile and were "descended of *Chus*, the Sonne of cursed *Cham*; as are all of that complexion."

As suggested by Sandys's remark, an equation had developed between African Negroes and slavery. Primarily, the associations were with the Portuguese and Spanish, with captivity, with buying and selling in Guinea and in America. While the Negro's exact status in America was not entirely clear, neither was it conceived as an off-brand of apprenticeship or servitude: Hawkins assumed as his crest a "demi-Moor" (plainly Negroid) "captive and bound." Nor was Portuguese or Spanish slavery regarded as being of a mild, protective sort:

The Portugals doe marke them as we doe Sheepe with a hot Iron, which the Moores call Crimbo, the poore slaves stand all in a row . . . and sing Mundele que sumbela he Carey ha belelelle, and thus the poore rogues are beguiled, for the Portugals make them beleeve that they that have not the marke is not accounted a man of any account in Brasil or in Portugall, and thos they bring the poore Moores to be in a most damnable bondage under the colour of love.

Englishmen had no special wish to emulate their rivals in these cruelties, unless like Hawkins they could silently profit by raiding some villages and furnishing transportation. There is no reason to suppose Englishmen eager to enslave Negroes, nor even to regard Richard Jobson eccentric in his response to a chief's offer to buy some "slaves": "I made answer, We were a people, who did not deale in any such commodities, neither did wee buy or sell one another, or any that had our owne shapes." By the seventeenth century, after all, English prejudices as well as English law were *in favorem libertatis*.

When they came to settle in America, Englishmen found that things happened to liberty, some favorable, some not. Negroes became slaves, partly because there were social and economic necessities in America which called for some sort of bound, controlled labor. The Portuguese and Spanish had set an example, which, however rough in outline, proved to be, at very least, suggestive to Englishmen. It would be surprising if there had been a clear-cut line of influence from Latin to English slavery. Elizabethans were not in the business of modeling themselves after Spaniards. Yet from about 1550, Englishmen were in such continual contact with the Spanish that they could hardly have failed to acquire the notion that Negroes could be enslaved. Precisely what slavery *meant*, of course, was a matter of English preconceptions patterning the information from overseas, but from the first, Englishmen tended to associate, in a diffuse way, Negroes with the Portuguese and Spanish. The term *negro* itself was incorporated into English from the Hispanic languages in mid-sixteenth century and *mulatto* a half century later. This is the more striking because a perfectly adequate term, identical in meaning to *negro*, already existed in English; of course *black* was used also, though not so commonly in the sixteenth century as later.

The fashion in which this absorption of foreign values took place may be illustrated by a remarkable passage in a book by a well-known Puritan theologian, Paul Baynes, who died in 1617, two years before the first Negroes arrived in the English colonies. Except for the four words set here in italics, his remarks were commonplace.

Now servants are either more slavish, or else more free and liberall: the first are such whose bodies are perpetually put under the power of the Master, *as Blackmores with us;* of which kinds servants are made sometime forcibly, as in captivity: sometime voluntarily, as when one doth willingly make himselfe over: sometime naturally, as the children of servants are borne the slaves of their Masters; and this [following type] was the most frequent kinde of service, wherein parties are upon certaine termes or conditions for a certaine time onely under the power of a man: such are our Apprentices, Journeymen, maideservants, etc.

Here, Negroes were incorporated casually into a thoroughly conventional discussion of age-old categories of servitude. His use of Negroes to illustrate a traditional category of bound labor would not have been possible much earlier. Baynes knew, as everyone did, that the "more slavish" variety of servitude had disappeared in England.

Actually, it is possible that someone else added the "blackmores" to Bayne's remarks after his death in 1617. In this period sermons were sometimes published with the speaker's original notes as the only basis for the final text, and the colossal tome which contains this passage was not published until the early 1640's. It is possible, therefore, that "as Blackmores with us" reflected more than an accidental spark struck off by English contact with the Hispanic world. For by 1640 it was becoming apparent that in many of the new colonies overseas the English settlers had obtained Negroes and were holding them, frequently, as hereditary slaves for life.

In considering the development of slavery in various groups of colonies, the above passage of (if not by) Paul Baynes can serve as a summary of the most essential features of the Negro's status as a slave. As the passage suggests, that status was at first distinguished from servitude more by duration than by oner-

ousness; the key term in this and in many other early descriptions of the Negro's condition was *perpetual*. Negroes served "for ever" and so would their children. Englishmen did not do so. Despite his conflation of the terms *servant* and *slave,* Baynes clearly differentiated the two statuses, and in this his thinking was typical. Servitude, no matter how long, brutal, and involuntary, was not the same thing as perpetual slavery. Servitude comprehended alike the young apprentice, the orphan, the indentured servant, the redemptioner, the convicted debtor or criminal, the political prisoner, and, even, the Scottish and Irish captive of war who was sold as a "slave" to New England or Barbados. Yet none of these persons, no matter how miserably treated, served for life in the colonies, though of course many died before their term ended. Hereditary lifetime service was restricted to Indians and Negroes. Among the various English colonies in the New World, this service known as "slavery" seems first to have developed in the international cockpit known as the Caribbean.

ENSLAVEMENT: THE WEST INDIES

The Englishmen who settled the Caribbean colonies were not very different from those who went to Virginia, Bermuda, Maryland, or even New England. Their experience in the islands, however, was very different indeed. By 1640 there were roughly as many English in the little islands as on the American continent. A half century after the first settlements were established in the 1620's, the major islands—Barbados, St. Kitts and the other Leeward Islands—were overcrowded. Thousands of whites who had been squeezed off the land by burgeoning sugar plantations migrated to other English colonies, including much larger Jamaica which had been captured from the Spanish in 1655. Their places were taken by Negro slaves who had been shipped to the islands, particularly after 1640, to meet an insatiable demand for labor which was cheap to maintain, easy to dragoon, and simple to replace when worked to death. Negroes outnumbered whites in Barbados as early as 1660. This rapid and thorough commitment to slavery placed white settlers under an ever-present danger of slave rebellion (the first rising came in 1638 on Providence Island), and whereas in the very early years authorities had rightly been fearful of white servant revolt, by the 1670's they were casting about desperately for means to attract white servants as protection against foreign and servile attack. Negro slavery matured hothouse fashion in the islands.

This compression of development was most clearly evident in the Puritan colony on the tiny island of Providence 150 miles off the coast of Central America, first settled in 1629 though not a going concern for several years. During the brief period before the Spanish snuffed out the colony in 1641 the settlers bought so many Negroes that white men were nearly outnumbered, and in England the Providence Company, apprehensive over possible Negro uprisings (with good reason as it turned out), drew up regulations for restricting the ratio of slaves to white men, "well knowing that if all men be left at Libty to buy as they please no man will take of English servants." Not only were Negroes cheaper to maintain but it was felt that they could legitimately be treated in a different way from Englishmen—they could be held to service for life. At least this was the impression prevailing among officials of the Providence Company in London, for in 1638 they wrote Governor Nathaniel Butler and the Council, "We also think it reasonable that whereas the English servants are to answer XX [pounds of tobacco] per head the Negros being procured at Cheaper rates more easily kept as perpetuall servants should answer 40 [pounds of tobacco] per head. And the rather that the desire of English bodyes may be kept, we are depending upon them for the defence of the Island. We shall also expect that Negroes performe service in the publique works in double proporcon to the English."

In Barbados this helpful idea that Negroes served for life seems to have existed even before they were purchased

in large numbers. In 1627 the ship bearing the first eighty settlers captured a prize from which ten Negroes were seized, so white men and Negroes settled the island together. Any doubt which may have existed as to the appropriate status of Negroes was dispelled in 1636 when Governor Henry Hawley and the Council resolved "that *Negroes* and *Indians,* that came here to be sold, should serve for Life, unless a Contract was before made to the contrary." Europeans were not treated in this manner: in 1643 Governor Philip Bell set at liberty fifty Portuguese who had been captured in Brazil and then offered for sale to Barbadians by a Dutch ship. The Governor seems to have been shocked by the proposed sale of Christian white men. In the 1650's several observers referred to the lifetime slavery of Negroes as if it were a matter of common knowledge. "Its the Custome for a Christian servant to serve foure yeares," one wrote at the beginning of the decade, "and then enjoy his freedome; and (which hee hath dearly earned) 10£ Ster. or the value of it in goods if his Master bee soe honest as to pay it; the Negros and Indians (of which latter there are but few here) they and the generation are Slaves to their owners to perpetuity." The widely read Richard Ligon wrote in 1657: "The Iland is divided into three sorts of men, *viz.* Masters, Servants, and slaves. The slaves and their posterity, being subject to their Masters for ever, are kept and preserv'd with greater care then the servants, who are theirs but for five yeers, according to the law of the Iland.". . .

The rapid introduction of Negro slavery into the English islands was accomplished without leaving any permanent trace of hesitation or misgivings. This was not the case in many of the continental colonies, both because different geographic and economic conditions prevailed there and because these conditions permitted a more complete and successful transplantation of English ways and values. This difference was particularly pronounced in New England, and it was therefore particularly ironic that the treatment accorded Negroes in New

England seems to have been directly influenced by the West Indian model.

ENSLAVEMENT: NEW ENGLAND

Negro slavery never really flourished in New England. It never became so important or so rigorous as in the plantation colonies to the southwards. There were relatively few Negroes, only a few hundred in 1680 and not more than 3 per cent of the population in the eighteenth century; no one thought that Negroes were about to rise and overwhelm the white community. Treatment of slaves in New England was milder even than the laws allowed: Negroes were not employed in gangs except occasionally in the Narragansett region of Rhode Island, and the established codes of family, congregation, and community mitigated the condition of servitude generally. Negroes were not treated very differently from white servants—except that somehow they and their children served for life.

The question with New England slavery is not why it was weakly rooted, but why it existed at all. No staple crop demanded regiments of raw labor. That there was no compelling economic demand for Negroes is evident in the numbers actually imported: economic exigencies scarcely required establishment of a distinct status for only 3 per cent of the labor force. Indentured servitude was adequate to New England's needs, and in fact some Negroes became free servants rather than slaves. Why, then, did New Englanders enslave Negroes, probably as early as 1638? Why was it that the Puritans rather mindlessly (which was not their way) accepted slavery for Negroes and Indians but not for white men?

The early appearance of slavery in New England may in part be explained by the provenance of the first Negroes imported. They were brought by Captain William Peirce of the Salem ship *Desire* in 1638 from the Providence Island colony where Negroes were already being kept as perpetual servants. A minor traffic in Negroes and other products developed between the two Puritan colonies, though evidently some of the Negroes

proved less than satisfactory, for Governor Butler was cautioned by the Providence Company to take special care of "the cannibal negroes brought from New England." After 1640 a brisk trade got under way between New England and the other English islands, and Massachusetts vessels sometimes touched upon the West African coast before heading for the Caribbean. Trade with Barbados was particularly lively, and Massachusetts vessels carried Negroes to that bustling colony from Africa and the Cape Verde Islands. . . . These strange Negroes from the West Indies must surely have been accompanied by prevailing notions about their usual status. Ship masters who purchased perpetual service in Barbados would not have been likely to sell service for term in Boston. Then too, white settlers from the crowded islands migrated to New England, 1,200 from Barbados alone in the years 1643–47.

No amount of contact with the West Indies could have by itself created Negro slavery in New England; settlers there had to be willing to accept the proposition. Because they were Englishmen, they were so prepared—and at the same time they were not. Characteristically, as Puritans, they officially codified this ambivalence in 1641 as follows: "there shall never be any bond-slavery, villenage or captivitie amongst us; unlesse it be lawfull captives taken in just warrs, and such strangers as willingly sell themselves, or are solde to us: and such shall have the libertyes and christian usages which the law of God established in Israell concerning such persons doth morally require, provided, this exempts none from servitude who shall be judged thereto by Authoritie." Here were the wishes of the General Court as expressed in the Massachusetts Body of Liberties, which is to say that as early as 1641 the Puritan settlers were seeking to guarantee in writing their own liberty without closing off the opportunity of taking it from others whom they identified with the Biblical term, "strangers." It was under the aegis of this concept that Theophilus Eaton, one of the founders of New Haven, seems to have owned Negroes before 1658 who were "servants forever or during his pleasure, according to Leviticus, 25:45 and 46." ("Of the children of the strangers that do sojourn among you, of them shall ye buy, and of their families . . . : and they shall be your possession. And ye shall take them as an inheritance for your children . . . ; they shall be your bondmen for ever: but over your brethren the children of Israel, ye shall not rule one over another with rigor.") Apart from this implication that bond slavery was reserved to those not partaking of true religion nor possessing proper nationality, the Body of Liberties expressly reserved the colony's right to enslave convicted criminals. For reasons not clear, this endorsement of an existing practice was followed almost immediately by discontinuance of its application to white men. The first instance of penal "slavery" in Massachusetts came in 1636, when an Indian was sentenced to "bee kept as a slave for life to worke, unles wee see further cause." Then in December 1638, ten months after the first Negroes arrived, the Quarter Court for the first time sentenced three white offenders to be "slaves"—a suggestive but perhaps meaningless coincidence. Having by June 1642 sentenced altogether some half dozen white men to "slavery" (and explicitly releasing several after less than a year) the Court stopped. Slavery, as had been announced in the Body of Liberties, was to be only for "strangers."

The Body of Liberties made equally clear that captivity in a just war constituted legitimate grounds for slavery. The practice had begun during the first major conflict with the Indians, the Pequot War of 1637. Some of the Pequot captives had been shipped aboard the *Desire,* to Providence Island; accordingly, the first Negroes in New England arrived in exchange for men taken captive in a just war! That this provenance played an important role in shaping views about Negroes is suggested by the first recorded plea by an Englishman on the North American continent for the establishment of an African slave trade. Emanuel Downing, in a letter to his brother-in-law John Winthrop in 1645, described the advantages: "If upon a Just warre [with the Narragansett Indians] the Lord should deliver them into our hands, wee might easily have men woemen and children enough to exchange for Moores, which wilbe more gaynefull pilladge for us then wee conceive, for I doe not see how wee can thrive untill wee get into a stock of slaves sufficient to doe all our buisiness, for our children's children will hardly see this great Continent filled with people, soe that our servants will still desire freedome to plant for themselves, and not stay but for verie great wages. And I suppose you know verie well how wee shall mayneteyne 20 Moores cheaper than one Englishe servant."

These two facets of justifiable enslavement—punishment for crime and captivity in war—were closely related. Slavery as punishment probably derived from analogy with captivity, since presumably a king or magistrates could mercifully spare and enslave a man whose crime had forfeited his right to life. The analogy had not been worked out by commentators in England, but a fairly clear linkage between crime and captivity seems to have existed in the minds of New Englanders concerning Indian slavery. In 1644 the commissioners of the United Colonies meeting at New Haven decided, in light of the Indians' "proud affronts," "hostile practices," and "protectinge or rescuinge of offenders," that magistrates might "send some convenient strength of English and, . . . seise and bring away" Indians from any "plantation of Indians" which persisted in this practice and, if no satisfaction was forthcoming, could deliver the "Indians seased . . . either to serve or be shipped out and exchanged for Negroes." Captivity and criminal justice seemed to mean the same thing, slavery.

It would be wrong to suppose that all the Puritans' preconceived ideas about freedom and bondage worked in the same direction. While the concepts of difference in religion and of captivity worked against Indians and Negroes, certain Scriptural injunctions and English pride in liberty told in the opposite direction. In Massachusetts the magistrates demonstrated that they were not about to tolerate glaring breaches of "the Law of God established in Israel" even when the victims were Negroes. In 1646 the authorities arrested two mariners, James Smith and Thomas Keyser, who had carried two Negroes directly from Africa and sold them in Massachusetts. What distressed the General Court was that the Negroes had been obtained during a raid on an African village and that this "haynos and crying sinn of man stealing" had transpired on the Lord's Day. The General Court decided to free the unfortunate victims and ship them back to Africa, though the death penalty for the crime (clearly mandatory in Scripture) was not imposed. More quietly than in this dramatic incident, Puritan authorities extended the same protections against maltreatment to Negroes and Indians as to white servants.

Only once before the eighteenth century was New England slavery challenged directly, and in that instance the tone was as much bafflement as indignation. This famous Rhode Island protest perhaps derived from a diffuse Christian equalitarianism which operated to extend the English presumption of liberty to non-Englishmen. The Rhode Island law of 1652 actually forbade enslavement. . . . Perhaps it was Rhode Island's tolerance of religious diversity and relatively high standard of justice for the Indian which led to this attempt to prevent Englishmen from taking advantage of a different people.

The law remained a dead letter. The need for labor, the example set in the West Indies, the condition of Negroes as "strangers," and their initial connection with captive Indians combined to override any hesitation about introducing Negro bond slavery into New England. Laws regulating the conduct of Negroes specifically did not appear until the 1690's. From the first, however, there were scattered signs that Negroes were regarded as different from English people not merely in their status as slaves. In 1639 Samuel Maverick of Noddles Island attempted, apparently rather clumsily, to breed two of his Negroes. . . . In 1652 the Massachusetts General

Court ordered that Scotsmen, Indians, and Negroes should train with the English in the militia, but four years later abruptly excluded Negroes, as did Connecticut in 1660. Evidently Negroes, even free Negroes, were regarded as distinct from the English. They were, in New England where economic necessities were not sufficiently pressing to determine the decision, treated differently from other men.

ENSLAVEMENT: VIRGINIA AND MARYLAND

In Virginia and Maryland the development of Negro slavery followed a very different course, for several reasons. Most obviously, geographic conditions and the intentions of the settlers quickly combined to produce a successful agricultural staple. The deep tidal rivers, the long growing season, the fertile soil, and the absence of strong communal spirit among the settlers opened the way. Ten years after settlers first landed at Jamestown they were on the way to proving, in the face of assertions to the contrary, that it was possible "to found an empire upon smoke." More than the miscellaneous productions of New England, tobacco required labor which was cheap but not temporary, mobile but not independent, and tireless rather than skilled. In the Chesapeake area more than anywhere to the northward, the shortage of labor and the abundance of land—the "frontier"—placed a premium on involuntary labor.

This need for labor played more directly upon these settlers' ideas about freedom and bondage than it did either in the West Indies or in New England. Perhaps it would be more accurate to say that settlers in Virginia (and in Maryland after settlement in 1634) made their decisions concerning Negroes while relatively virginal, relatively free from external influences and from firm preconceptions. Of all the important early English settlements, Virginia had the least contact with the Spanish, Portuguese, Dutch, and other English colonies. At the same time, the settlers of Virginia did not possess either the legal or Scriptural learning of the New England Puritans whose conception of the just war had opened the way to the enslavement of Indians. Slavery in the tobacco colonies did not begin as an adjunct of captivity; in marked contrast to the Puritan response to the Pequot War the settlers of Virginia did *not* generally react to the Indian massacre of 1622 with propositions for taking captives and selling them as "slaves." It was perhaps a correct measure of the conceptual atmosphere in Virginia that there was only one such proposition after the 1622 disaster and that that one was defective in precision as to how exactly one treated captive Indians.

In the absence, then, of these influences which obtained in other English colonies, slavery as it developed in Virginia and Maryland assumes a special interest and importance over and above the fact that Negro slavery was to become a vitally important institution there and, later, to the southwards. In the tobacco colonies it is possible to watch Negro slavery *develop,* not pop up full-grown overnight, and it is therefore possible to trace, very imperfectly, the development of the shadowy, unexamined rationale which supported it. The concept of Negro slavery there was neither borrowed from foreigners, nor extracted from books, nor invented out of whole cloth, nor extrapolated from servitude, nor generated by English reaction to Negroes as such, nor necessitated by the exigencies of the New World. Not any one of these made the Negro a slave, but all.

In rough outline, slavery's development in the tobacco colonies seems to have undergone three stages. Negroes first arrived in 1619, only a few days late for the meeting of the first representative assembly in America. John Rolfe described the event with the utmost unconcern: "About the last of August came in a dutch man of warre that sold us twenty Negars." Negroes continued to trickle in slowly for the next half century; one report in 1649 estimated that there were three hundred among Virginia's population of fifteen thousand —about 2 per cent. Long before there were more appreciable numbers, the de-

velopment of slavery had, so far as we can tell, shifted gears. Prior to about 1640, there is very little evidence to show how Negroes were treated—though we will need to return to those first twenty years in a moment. After 1640 there is mounting evidence that some Negroes were in fact being treated as slaves, at least that they were being held in hereditary lifetime service. This is to say that the twin essences of slavery—the two kinds of perpetuity—first become evident during the twenty years prior to the beginning of legal formulation. After 1660 slavery was written into statute law. Negroes began to flood into the two colonies at the end of the seventeenth century. In 1705 Virginia produced a codification of laws applying to slaves.

Concerning the first of these stages, there is only one major historical certainty, and unfortunately it is the sort which historians find hardest to bear. There simply is not enough evidence to indicate with any certainty whether Negroes were treated like white servants or not. At least we can be confident, therefore, that the two most common assertions about the first Negroes—that they were slaves and that they were servants —are *unfounded,* though not necessarily incorrect. And what of the positive evidence?

Some of the first group bore Spanish names and presumably had been baptized, which would mean they were at least nominally Christian, though of the Papist sort. They had been "sold" to the English; so had other Englishmen but not by the Dutch. Certainly these Negroes were not fully free, but many Englishmen were not. It can be said, though, that from the first in Virginia Negroes were set apart from white men by the word *Negroes.* The earliest Virginia census reports plainly distinguished Negroes from white men, often giving Negroes no personal name; in 1629 every commander of the several plantations was ordered to "take a generall muster of all the inhabitants men woemen and Children as well *Englishe* as Negroes." A distinct name is not attached to a group unless it is regarded as distinct. It seems logical to suppose that this perception of the Negro as being distinct from the Englishman must have operated to debase his status rather than to raise it, for in the absence of countervailing social factors, the need for labor in the colonies usually told in the direction of non-freedom. There were few countervailing factors present, surely, in such instances as in 1629 when a group of Negroes were brought to Virginia freshly captured from a Portuguese vessel which had snatched them from Angola a few weeks earlier. Given the context of English thought and experience sketched in this chapter, it seems probable that the Negro's status was not ever the same as that accorded the white servant. But we do not know for sure.

When the first fragmentary evidence appears about 1640 it becomes clear that *some* Negroes in both Virginia and Maryland were serving for life and some Negro children inheriting the same obligation. Not all Negroes, certainly, for Nathaniel Littleton had released a Negro named Anthony Longoe from all service whatsoever in 1635, and after the mid-1640's the court records show that other Negroes were incontestably free and were accumulating property of their own. At least one Negro freeman, Anthony Johnson, himself owned a Negro. Some Negroes served only terms of usual length, but others were held for terms far longer than custom and statute permitted with white servants. The first fairly clear indication that slavery was practiced in the tobacco colonies appears in 1639, when a Maryland statute declared that "all the Inhabitants of this Province being Christians (slaves excepted) Shall have and enjoy all such rights liberties immunities priviledges and free customs within this Province as any naturall born subject of England." Another Maryland law passed the same year provided that "all persons being Christians (Slaves excepted)" over eighteen who were imported without indentures would serve for four years. These laws make very little sense unless the term *slaves* meant Negroes and perhaps Indians.

The next year, 1640, the first definite indication of outright enslavement appears in Virginia. The General Court pronounced sentence on three servants who had been retaken after absconding to Maryland. Two of them, a Dutchman and a Scot, were ordered to serve their masters for one additional year and then the colony for three more, but "the third being a negro named John Punch shall serve his said master or his assigns for the time of his natural life here or else where." No white servant in any English colony, so far as is known, ever received a like sentence. Later the same month a Negro (possibly the same enterprising fellow) was again singled out from a group of recaptured runaways; six of the seven culprits were assigned additional time while the Negro was given none, presumably because he was already serving for life.

After 1640, when surviving Virginia county court records began to mention Negroes, sales for life, often including any future progeny, were recorded in unmistakable language. In 1646 Francis Pott sold a Negro woman and boy to Stephen Charlton "to the use of him . . . forever." Similarly, six years later William Whittington sold to John Pott "one Negro girle named Jowan; aged about Ten yeares and with her Issue and produce duringe her (or either of them) for their Life tyme. And their Successors forever"; and a Maryland man in 1649 deeded two Negro men and a woman "and all their issue both male and Female." . . .

Further evidence that some Negroes were serving for life in this period lies in the prices paid for them. In many instances the valuations placed on Negroes (in estate inventories and bills of sale) were far higher than for white servants, even those servants with full terms yet to serve. Higher prices must have meant that Negroes were more highly valued because of their greater length of service. Negro women may have been especially prized, moreover, because their progeny could also be held perpetually. In 1643, for example, William Burdett's inventory listed eight servants, with the time each had still to serve, at valuations ranging from 400 to 1,100 pounds of tobacco, while a "very anntient" Negro was valued at 3,000 and an eight-year-old Negro girl at 2,000 pounds, with no time remaining indicated for either. In the late 1650's an inventory of Thomas Ludlow's estate evaluated a white servant with six years to serve at less than an elderly Negro man and only one half of a Negro woman. . . . Besides setting a higher value on Negroes these inventories failed to indicate the number of years they had still to serve, presumably because their service was for an unlimited time.

Where Negro women were involved, higher valuations probably reflected the facts that their issue were valuable and that they could be used for field work while white women generally were not. The latter discrimination between Negro and white women did not necessarily involve perpetual service, but it meant that Negroes were set apart in a way clearly not to their advantage. This was not the only instance in which Negroes were subjected to degrading distinctions not immediately and necessarily attached to the concept of slavery. Negroes were singled out for special treatment in several ways which suggest a generalized debasement of Negroes as a group. Significantly, the first indications of this debasement appeared at about the same time as the first indications of actual enslavement.

The distinction concerning field work is a case in point. It first appears on the written record in 1643, when Virginia almost pointedly endorsed it in a tax law. Previously, in 1629, tithable persons had been defined as "all those that worke in the ground of what qualitie or condition soever." The new law provided that *all* adult men were tithable and, in addition, *Negro* women. The same distinction was made twice again before 1660. Maryland adopted a similar policy beginning in 1654. This official discrimination between Negro and other women was made by men who were accustomed to thinking of field work as being ordinarily the work of men rather than women. . . . The essentially racial character of this discrimination stood out clearly in a law passed in 1668 at the

time slavery was taking shape in the statute books:

Whereas some doubts, have arisen whether negro women set free were still to be accompted tithable according to a former act, *It is declared by this grand assembly* that negro women, though permitted to enjoy their Freedome yet ought not in all respects to be admitted to a full fruition of the exemptions and impunities of the English, and are still lyable to payment of taxes.

Virginia law set Negroes apart from all other groups in a second way by denying them the important right and obligation to bear arms. Few restraints could indicate more clearly the denial to Negroes of membership in the white community. This first foreshadowing of the slave codes came in 1640, at just the time when other indications first appeared that Negroes were subject to special treatment.

Finally, an even more compelling sense of the separateness of Negroes was revealed in early reactions to sexual union between the races. Prior to 1660 the evidence concerning these reactions is equivocal, and it is not possible to tell whether repugnance for intermixture preceded legislative enactment of slavery. In 1630 an angry Virginia court sentenced "Hugh Davis to be soundly whipped, before an assembly of Negroes and others for abusing himself to the dishonor of God and shame of Christians, by defiling his body in lying with a negro," but it is possible that the "negro" may not have been female. With other instances of punishment for interracial union in the ensuing years, fornication rather than miscegenation may well have been the primary offense, though in 1651 a Maryland man sued someone who he claimed had said "that he had a black bastard in Virginia.". . . A quarter century later in 1676, however, the emergence of distaste for racial intermixture was unmistakable. A contemporary account of Bacon's Rebellion caustically described one of the ringleaders, Richard Lawrence, as a person who had eclipsed his learning and abilities "in the darke imbraces of a Blackamoore, his slave: And that in so fond a

Maner, . . . to the noe meane Scandle and affrunt of all the Vottrisses in or about towne."

Such condemnation was not confined to polemics. In the early 1660's when slavery was gaining statutory recognition, the assemblies acted with full-throated indignation against miscegenation. These acts aimed at more than merely avoiding confusion of status. In 1662 Virginia declared that "if any christian shall committ Fornication with a negro man or woman, hee or shee soe offending" should pay double the usual fine. (The next year Bermuda prohibited all sexual relations between whites and Negroes.) Two years later Maryland banned interracial marriages. . . . A Maryland act of 1681 described marriages of white women with Negroes as, among other things, "always to the Satisfaccion of theire Lascivious and Lustfull desires, and to the disgrace not only of the English butt allso of many other Christian Nations." When Virginia finally prohibited all interracial liaisons in 1691, the Assembly vigorously denounced miscegenation and its fruits as "that abominable mixture and spurious issue."

From the surviving evidence, it appears that outright enslavement and these other forms of debasement appeared at about the same time in Maryland and Virginia. Indications of perpetual service, the very nub of slavery, coincided with indications that English settlers discriminated against Negro women, withheld arms from Negroes, and—though the timing is far less certain—reacted unfavorably to interracial sexual union. The coincidence suggests a mutual relationship between slavery and unfavorable assessment of Negroes. Rather than slavery causing "prejudice," or vice versa, they seem rather to have generated each other. Both were, after all, twin aspects of a general debasement of the Negro. Slavery and "prejudice" may have been equally cause and effect, continuously reacting upon each other, dynamically joining hands to hustle the Negro down the road to complete degradation. Much more than with the other English colonies, where the en-

slavement of Negroes was to some extent a borrowed practice, the available evidence for Maryland and Virginia points to less borrowing and to this kind of process: a mutually interactive growth of slavery and unfavorable assessment, with no cause for either which did not cause the other as well. If slavery caused prejudice, then invidious distinctions concerning working in the fields, bearing arms, and sexual union should have appeared *after* slavery's firm establishment. If prejudice caused slavery, then one would expect to find these lesser discriminations preceding the greater discrimination of outright enslavement. Taken as a whole, the evidence reveals a process of debasement of which hereditary lifetime service was an important but not the only part.

White servants did not suffer this debasement. Rather, their position improved, partly for the reason that they were not Negroes. By the early 1660's white men were loudly protesting against being made "slaves" in terms which strongly suggest that they considered slavery not as wrong but as inapplicable to themselves. . . . Free Negro servants were generally increasingly less able to defend themselves against this insidious kind of encroachment. Increasingly, white men were more clearly free because Negroes had become so clearly slave.

Certainly it was the case in Maryland and Virginia that the legal enactment of Negro slavery followed social practice, rather than vice versa, and also that the assemblies were slower than in other English colonies to declare how Negroes could or should be treated. These two patterns in themselves suggest that slavery was less a matter of previous conception or external example in Maryland and Virginia than elsewhere.

The Virginia Assembly first showed itself incontrovertibly aware that Negroes were not serving in the same manner as English servants in 1660 when it declared "that for the future no servant comeing into the country without indentures, of what christian nation soever, shall serve longer then those of our own country, of the like age." In 1661 the

Assembly indirectly provided statutory recognition that some Negroes served for life: "That in case any English servant shall run away in company with any negroes who are incapable of makeing satisfaction by addition of time," he must serve for the Negroes' lost time as well as his own. Maryland enacted a closely similar law in 1663 (possibly modeled on Virginia's) and in the following year, on the initiative of the lower house, came out with the categorical declaration that Negroes were to serve "Durante Vita." During the next twenty-odd years a succession of acts in both colonies defined with increasing precision what sorts of persons might be treated as slaves. Other acts dealt with the growing problem of slave control, and especially after 1690 slavery began to assume its now familiar character as a complete deprivation of all rights. As early as 1669 the Virginia Assembly unabashedly enacted a brutal law which showed where the logic of perpetual servitude was inevitably tending. Unruly servants could be chastened by sentences to additional terms, but "WHEREAS the only law in force for the punishment of refractory servants resisting their master, mistris or overseer cannot be inflicted upon negroes, nor the obstinacy of many of them by other then violent meanes supprest," if a slave "by the extremity of the correction should chance to die" his master was not to be adjudged guilty of felony "since it cannot be presumed that prepensed malice (which alone makes murther Felony) should induce any man to destroy his owne estate." Virginia planters felt they acted out of mounting necessity: there were disturbances among slaves in several areas in the early 1670's.

By about 1700 the slave ships began spilling forth their black cargoes in greater and greater numbers. By that time, racial slavery and the necessary police powers had been written into law. By that time, too, slavery had lost all resemblance to a perpetual and hereditary version of English servitude, though service for life still seemed to contemporaries its most essential feature. In the last quarter of the seventeenth century the trend was to treat Negroes more like property and less like men, to send them to the fields at younger ages, to deny them automatic existence as inherent members of the community, to tighten the bonds on their personal and civil freedom, and correspondingly to loosen the traditional restraints on the master's freedom to deal with his human property as he saw fit. In 1705 Virginia gathered up the random statutes of a whole generation and baled them into a "slave code" which would not have been out of place in the nineteenth century.

* * *

RACIAL SLAVERY: FROM REASONS TO RATIONALE

Difference, surely, was the indispensable key to the degradation of Negroes in English America. In scanning the problem of *why* Negroes were enslaved in America, certain constant elements in a complex situation can be readily, if roughly, identified. It may be taken as given that there would have been no enslavement without economic need, that is, without persistent demand for labor in underpopulated colonies. Of crucial importance, too, was the fact that for cultural reasons Negroes were relatively helpless in the face of European aggressiveness and technology. In themselves, however, these two elements will not explain the enslavement of Indians and Negroes. The pressing exigency in America was labor, and Irish and English servants were available. Most of them would have been helpless to ward off outright enslavement if their masters had thought themselves privileged and able to enslave them. As a group, though, masters did not think themselves so empowered. Only with Indians and Negroes did Englishmen attempt so radical a deprivation of liberty—which brings the matter abruptly to the most difficult and imponderable question of all: what was it about Indians and Negroes which set them apart, which rendered them *different* from Englishmen, which made them special candidates for degradation?

To ask such questions is to inquire into the *content* of English attitudes, and unfortunately there is little evidence with which to build an answer. It may be said, however, that the heathen condition of the Negroes seemed of considerable importance to English settlers in America—more so than to English voyagers upon the coasts of Africa—and that heathenism was associated in some settlers' minds with the condition of slavery. This is not to say that the colonists enslaved Negroes because they were heathens. . . .

The importance and persistence of the tradition which attached slavery to heathenism did not become evident in any positive assertions that heathens might be enslaved. It was not until the period of legal establishment of slavery after 1660 that the tradition became manifest at all, and even then there was no effort to place heathenism and slavery on a one-for-one relationship. Virginia's second statutory definition of a slave (1682), for example, awkwardly attempted to rest enslavement on religious difference while excluding from possible enslavement all heathens who were not Indian or Negro. Despite such logical difficulties, the old European equation of slavery and religious difference did not rapidly vanish in America, for it cropped up repeatedly after 1660 in assertions that slaves by becoming Christian did not automatically become free. By about the end of the seventeenth century, Maryland, New York, Virginia, North and South Carolina, and New Jersey had all passed laws reassuring masters that conversion of their slaves did not necessitate manumission. These acts were passed in response to occasional pleas that Christianity created a claim to freedom and to much more frequent assertions by men interested in converting Negroes that nothing could be accomplished if masters thought their slaves were about to be snatched from them by meddling missionaries. This decision that the slave's religious condition had no relevance to his status as a slave (the only one possible if an already valuable economic institution was to be retained) strongly suggests that heathenism was an important component in the

colonists' initial reaction to Negroes early in the century.

Yet its importance can easily be overstressed. For one thing, some of the first Negroes in Virginia had been baptized before arrival. In the early years others were baptized in various colonies and became more than nominally Christian; a Negro woman joined the church in Dorchester, Massachusetts, as a full member in 1641. With some Negroes becoming Christian and others not, there might have developed a caste differentiation along religious lines, yet there is no evidence to suggest that the colonists distinguished consistently between the Negroes they converted and those they did not. It was racial, not religious, slavery which developed in America.

Still, in the early years, the English settlers most frequently contrasted themselves with Negroes by the term *Christian*, though they also sometimes described themselves as *English;* here the explicit religious distinction would seem to have lain at the core of English reaction. Yet the concept embodied by the term *Christian* embraced so much more meaning than was contained in specific doctrinal affirmations that it is scarcely possible to assume on the basis of this linguistic contrast that the colonists set Negroes apart because they were heathen. The historical experience of the English people in the sixteenth century had made for fusion of religion and nationality; the qualities of being English and Christian had become so inseparably blended that it seemed perfectly consistent to the Virginia Assembly in 1670 to declare that "noe negroe or Indian though baptised and enjoyed their owne Freedome shall be capable of any such purchase of christians, but yet not debarred from buying any of their owne nation." Similarly, an order of the Virginia Assembly in 1662 revealed a well-knit sense of self-identity of which Englishness and Christianity were interrelated parts: "METAPPIN a Powhatan Indian being sold for life time to one Elizabeth Short by the king of Wainoake Indians who had no power to sell him being of another nation, *it is ordered* that the said Indian be free, he speaking perfectly the English tongue and desiring baptism."

From the first, then, vis-à-vis the Negro the concept embedded in the term *Christian* seems to have conveyed much of the idea and feeling of *we* as against *they*: to be Christian was to be civilized rather than barbarous, English rather than African, white rather than black. The term *Christian* itself proved to have remarkable elasticity, for by the end of the seventeenth century it was being used to define a species of slavery which had altogether lost any connection with explicit religious difference. In the Virginia code of 1705, for example, the term sounded much more like a definition of race than of religion: "And for a further christian care and usage of all christian servants, *Be it also enacted, by the authority aforesaid, and it is hereby enacted,* That no negroes, mulattos, or Indians, although christians, or Jews, Moors, Mahometans, or other infidels, shall, at any time, purchase any christian servant, nor any other, except of their own complexion, or such as are declared slaves by this act." By this time "Christianity" had somehow become intimately and explicitly linked with "complexion." . . . As late as 1753 the Virginia slave code anachronistically defined slavery in terms of religion when everyone knew that slavery had for generations been based on the racial and not the religious difference.

It is worth making still closer scrutiny of the terminology which Englishmen employed when referring both to themselves and to the two peoples they enslaved, for this terminology affords the best single means of probing the content of their sense of difference. The terms *Indian* and *Negro* were both borrowed from the Hispanic languages, the one originally deriving from (mistaken) geographical locality and the other from human complexion. When referring to the Indians the English colonists either used that proper name or called them *savages,* a term which reflected primarily their view of Indians as uncivilized, or occasionally (in Maryland especially)

pagans, which gave more explicit expression to the missionary urge. When they had reference to Indians the colonists occasionally spoke of themselves as *Christians* but after the early years almost always as *English.*

In significant contrast, the colonists referred to *Negroes* and by the eighteenth century to *blacks* and to *Africans,* but almost never to Negro *heathens* or *pagans* or *savages.* Most suggestive of all, there seems to have been something of a shift during the seventeenth century in the terminology which Englishmen in the colonies applied to themselves. From the initially most common term *Christian,* at mid-century there was a marked drift toward *English* and *free.* After about 1680, taking the colonies as a whole, a new term appeared— *white.*

So far as the weight of analysis may be imposed upon such terms, diminishing reliance upon *Christian* suggests a gradual muting of the specifically religious element in the Christian-Negro disjunction in favor of secular nationality: Negroes were, in 1667, "not in all respects to be admitted to a full fruition of the exemptions and impunities of the English." As time went on, as some Negroes became assimilated to the English colonial culture, as more "raw Africans" arrived, and as increasing numbers of non-English Europeans were attracted to the colonies, the colonists turned increasingly to the striking physiognomic difference. . . . Here was a barrier between "we" and "they" which was visible and permanent: the Negro could not become a white man. Not, at least, as yet. . . .

Whatever the limitations of terminology as an index to thought and feeling, it seems likely that the colonists' initial sense of difference from the Negro was founded not on a single characteristic but on a congeries of qualities which, taken as a whole, seemed to set the Negro apart. Virtually every quality in the Negro invited pejorative feelings. What may have been his two most striking characteristics, his heathenism and his appearance, were probably prerequisite

to his complete debasement. His heathenism alone could never have led to
permanent enslavement since conversion easily wiped out that failing. If his
appearance, his racial characteristics,
meant nothing to the English settlers, it
is difficult to see how slavery based on
race ever emerged, how the concept of
complexion as the mark of slavery ever
entered the colonists' minds. Even if the
colonists were most unfavorably struck
by the Negro's color, though, blackness
itself did not urge the complete debasement of slavery. Other qualities—the
utter strangeness of his language, ges-
tures, eating habits, and so on—certainly must have contributed to the colonists' sense that he was very different,
perhaps disturbingly so. In Africa these
qualities had for Englishmen added up
to *savagery;* they were major components in that sense of *difference* which
provided the mental margin absolutely
requisite for placing the European on
the deck of the slave ship and the Negro
in the hold.

The available evidence (what little
there is) suggests that for Englishmen
settling in America, the specific religious difference was initially of greater
importance than color, certainly of
much greater relative importance than
for the Englishmen who confronted Negroes in their African homeland. Perhaps Englishmen in Virginia, living un-
comfortably close to nature under a hot
sun and in almost daily contact with
tawny Indians, found the Negro's color
less arresting than they might have in
other circumstances. Perhaps, too, these
first Virginians sensed how inadequately
they had reconstructed the institutions
and practices of Christian piety in the
wilderness; they would perhaps appear
less as failures to themselves in this re-

spect if compared to persons who as
Christians were *totally* defective. In this
connection they may be compared to
their brethren in New England, where
godliness appeared (at first) trium-
phantly to hold full sway; in New England there was distinctly less contrasting of Negroes on the basis of the
religious disjunction and much more
militant discussion of just wars. Perhaps, though, the Jamestown settlers
were told in 1619 by the Dutch shipmas-
ter that these "negars" were heathens
and could be treated as such. We do not
know. The available data will not bear
all the weight that the really crucial
questions impose.

Of course once the cycle of degradation was fully under way, once slavery
and racial discrimination were completely linked together, once the engine
of oppression was in full operation, then
there is no need to plead *ignoramus.* By
the end of the seventeenth century in all
the colonies of the English empire there
was chattel racial slavery of a kind
which would have seemed familiar to
men living in the nineteenth century.
No Elizabethan Englishman would have
found it familiar, though certain strands
of thought and feeling in Elizabethan
England had intertwined with reports
about the Spanish and Portuguese to en-
gender a willingness on the part of English settlers in the New World to treat
some men as suitable for private exploitation. During the seventeenth century
New World conditions had exploited this
predisposition and vastly enlarged it, so
much so that English colonials of the
eighteenth century were faced with full-
blown slavery—something they thought
of not as an institution but as a host of
ever present problems, dangers, and opportunities.

II. THE DEVELOPMENT OF FORMAL INSTITUTIONS

Thad W. Tate

THE EIGHTEENTH CENTURY: THE GROWTH OF SLAVERY

COLONIAL BLACK CODES

The eighteenth century is frequently neglected in considering the development of slavery as scholars jump from the early years to the antebellum period. But as Tate's study illustrates, eighteenth-century events played a crucial part in establishing basic patterns of American behavior. Moreover his analysis reveals the complex relationship between economic interest and social attitudes. The rise of Black Codes further illustrates how slavery became a structure of social control as well as an economic system. Dr. Tate, editor of the *William and Mary Quarterly*, the leading journal of early American history, is a specialist in eighteenth-century Virginia history.

THE EIGHTEENTH CENTURY: THE GROWTH OF SLAVERY

THE 16,390 Negroes residing in Virginia in 1700 had grown to 26,559 by 1720, to 30,000 by 1730, or almost double the 1700 figure. In the next decade—the 1730's—the Negro population doubled once again, reaching an estimated 60,000. It was not long until annual importations of Negroes had climbed to a peak of three or four thousand a year, while the number of Virgian-born Negroes increased correspondingly.

By mid-century the estimates of population varied widely, but Governor Dinwiddie's 1756 figures were perhaps as reliable as any. Estimating from the count of tithables, he arrived at a total population in Virginia of 293,472, of which 173,316 were white and 120,156 Negro. By the 1760's the proportion of white to Negro was not quite half and half, a ratio which remained more or less constant to the end of the eighteenth century. As was to be expected, the highest density of Negroes occurred in the Tidewater, but slaves were also numerous in the Piedmont. Only in the Valley and in the mountain areas was the Negro population really small.

This rapid increase did not depend alone on the willingness of the colonial planters to employ Negro labor. It also demanded the evolution of an efficient, large-scale slave trade. Through much of the seventeenth century sporadic Dutch trading activity was responsible for most of the importations of Negroes. The Virginia Assembly attempted to encourage this trade in 1659 by exempting Dutch merchants from paying ten shillings per hogshead duty on tobacco received for Negroes, permitting them to pay instead the two shillings English duty.

English mercantile interests did not become actively involved in the African slave trade until the Restoration. In 1662 The Company of Royal Adventurers Trading to Africa received a monopoly of the slave trade. This company,

From Thad W. Tate, *The Negro in Eighteenth-Century Williamsburg* (Colonial Williamsburg, Inc., 1965) pp. 23–42. Reprinted by permission of Thad W. Tate, Colonial Williamsburg, Inc., and the University Press of Virginia.

however, survived for only ten difficult years and never recorded a contract for supplying Virginia with Negroes. In 1672 a new company, the Royal African Company, received a charter which passed along to it the monopoly of the slave trade to the English colonies. There has been a tendency to assume too easily that the company was able to take full advantage of its favored position. In reality, the Royal African Company found it difficult to protect itself against interlopers from both England and the colonies. Not even the support of the Crown, which consistently instructed royal governors to give all possible encouragement to the company, could help. The Royal African Company contracted on several occasions in the 1670's for shipments of Negroes to Virginia and made some deliveries. But, even though Governor Culpeper's statement that the company had never sold slaves in the colony was obviously an exaggeration, the Royal African Company was unsuccessful in dominating the Virginia market.

Some of the challengers of the company monopoly seemed to have established good local connections in Virginia through men like the first William Byrd and William Fitzhugh. In the 1680's Byrd was interested in a number of transactions that involved bringing in small shipments of Negroes from the West Indies. About the same time Fitzhugh was in correspondence with a New England merchant about the details of trading tobacco for slaves.

Ultimately, in 1698, the Royal African Company lost its monopoly, being forced to give way to an arrangement which permitted "separate traders" to carry slaves by paying certain duties to the company. Other merchants could now openly compete, sending their vessels, among other places, to the landings and ports which dotted the Virginia rivers. The figures for 1699–1708, which show that the separate traders carried 5,692 Negroes to Virginia and the Royal African Company 679, are a clear indication of the weak position of the Company in the trade. After these years shipments of slaves by the Company became increasingly intermittent, though there were still a few to Virginia in the 1720's. Then, after 1730, it no longer shipped Negroes from the African coast. The flow of slaves continued, however, with Bristol and Liverpool merchants dominating the trade. A sprinkling of New England vessels also brought slave cargoes from Africa, and a number of Virginia ships were employed to bring small groups of Negroes from the West Indies into the colony.

As the century progressed, new Negroes were sold farther and farther up the rivers, until settlements on the Fall Line like Rocky Ridge, across the James from Richmond, became the most important slave markets in the colony. There was also a domestic trade in Virginia-born Negroes, prized for their greater skill and adjustment to white civilization and therefore commanding higher prices.

As much as they had come to value slave labor, Virginians viewed these large-scale importations of Negroes with misgivings. No one has yet managed a completely satisfactory explanation of why the colonists began to wish they could put some limit on the number of slaves to be introduced into the colony. An older generation of Virginia historians claimed to find evidence of moral and humanitarian objections to the trade in human beings. Some of them have even charged that slaves were forced on the Southern colonies by the pressure of greedy British and New England mercantile groups. Any close reading of the evidence quickly suggests how little support there is for this point of view, whether it be the prevailing attitudes of most of the planters toward the Negro or in the fact that no cargo of healthy slaves ever lacked for purchasers. It is clear that much less idealistic reasons were responsible for the planters' objections.

For one thing, social control of the Negro played a large part in the increasing uneasiness of the whites. Fear of slave insurrection became a daily fact of life in Virginia, and ultimately the slave owners came to feel that there must be a limit beyond which the proportion of Negroes in the population could not safely go. An economic factor was also involved. Often the explanation has been that owners of Negroes already in Virginia had a speculative interest in keeping additional African Negroes out in order to assure a steady increase in the value of their own human property. What seems more convincing, however, is the fact that many planters opposed the further drain of money and increase in colonial indebtedness that the purchase of African slaves necessarily imposed. Prosperity in the slave trade was directly related to economic conditions of the tobacco market with the result that it suffered some of the same consequences of overextended credit. The more perceptive colonists were fully aware of the connection.

The principal stratagem which the leaders of the colony evolved for discouraging too rapid an increase in the number of slaves was an import duty on African slaves that could be disguised as a revenue measure. The long series of laws which enacted these duties began as early as 1699, and, for the first few years, were honestly intended to raise funds rather than discourage trade. The initial act, for example, levied a charge of twenty shillings for each Negro imported specifically for the construction of the new Capitol at Williamsburg. With one renewal this duty continued in force until late 1703. After a three month interval in early 1704 during which no duty was in effect, the impost was revived in April, 1704. From then until 1718 some form of duty was in force without an important break. The tendency to make the duties prohibitory in character also began to appear, for during these years the amount climbed as high as £5 per Negro.

From 1718 to 1723 the Assembly made no attempt to continue the duty. Then, in 1723 an attempt to restore it at the rate of 40 shillings touched off the first organized opposition from English traders. The flood of petitions and representations by these men carried enough political weight to persuade the King to disallow the 1723 law and all subsequent attempts of the Assembly to pass a duty over the next nine years.

By a change of tactics that made a 5% *ad valorem* duty payable by the prospective buyer rather than by the importer the General Assembly broke the deadlock in 1732. Thereafter and until the outbreak of the Revolution an *ad valorem* duty on slaves was in effect in Virginia, except for six months during 1751. The 5% rate of 1732 was gradually increased, until it stood at 20% during part of the French and Indian War. The whole effort to discourage the foreign slave trade led ultimately to the unsuccessful petition of the Assembly in 1772 for a complete end to further importations and to the successful prohibition of the trade by the new state government in 1778. But these events are more logically a part of the American Revolution in Virginia. Down to the outbreak of that struggle African slavers and West Indian traders continued to land their human cargoes in the colony with but little discouragement.

The role which the African Negroes and their American-born descendants assumed in plantation society possesses a certain familiarity. The fact that most histories of slavery leap so quickly to the nineteenth century, where the details of plantation life survive so much more abundantly, does place difficulties in the way of a full picture of the eighteenth. However, the general outlines of the work of the Negro slaves, of their daily existence, and of their immovable position at the bottom of a stratified colonial society seem clear enough.

The largest proportion of Negroes—men, women, and children—were field hands, assigned to growing tobacco and the other marketable crops the colony produced. This was the real purpose for which slavery had evolved, and it represented the institution in its most impersonal, burdensome, and typical form. The account of the field slave's lot by J. F. D. Smyth, an English traveller in Virginia just before the Revolution, is admittedly an unflattering one and no more to be accepted uncritically than any other single observation; but it is probably accurate enough in its description of the working day:

. . . He [the slave] is called up in the morning at day break, and is seldom allowed time enough to swallow three mouthfuls of hominy, or hoecake, but is driven out immediately to the field to hard labour, at which he continues, without intermission, until noon. . . . About noon is the time he eats his dinner, and he is seldom allowed an hour for that purpose. . . .

They [i.e., the slaves] then return to severe labour, which continues in the field until dusk in the evening, when they repair to the tobaccohouses, where each has his task in stripping alotted him, that employs him for some hours.

A smaller, but still significant number, of slaves fared somewhat better as household workers and personal servants of the master's family. Almost invariably accounts of slaves who enjoyed especially lenient treatment or some bond of affection from their masters refer to Negroes from the household staff. Even so, there has been an easy tendency to view this group of slaves in a romantic light, and there is much we really do not know about their life.

A third segment of the slave labor force was composed of skilled and semi-skilled craftsmen. In time Negroes performed substantially all of the work on plantations in certain trades, especially carpentry and cooperage. Frequently, they were also proficient millers, tanners, shoemakers, wheelwrights, spinners, and weavers. Not only did these slave artisans perform tasks necessary for individual plantations; they were also instrumental in the commercial development of the Southern colonies, especially in tanning, in the rudimentary iron industry which was developing, and in the preparation of lumber and staves for export.

There are not many extant lists of slaves which provide a specific breakdown of the division of labor on the plantation from which they came. There is one, however, for Green Spring Plantation in 1770, when the estate of its deceased owner, Philip Ludwell, was be-

ing settled. At that time Ludwell's son-in-law, William Lee, described the slaves at Green Spring as including 59 "crop Negroes," a figure which was "exclusive of boys"; 12 house servants; 4 carpenters; 1 wheelwright; 2 shoemakers; and 3 gardeners and hostlers.

It is easy to overestimate the number of slaves owned by an individual planter and even easier to miscalculate the number used to operate a single plantation or quarter. The eighty-odd Negroes at Green Spring were the largest single group from a combined total of 164 on all the lands belonging to Philip Ludwell's estate. This total was more than enough to mark Ludwell as one of the more substantial members of the planter aristocracy, as his membership on the Governor's Council also testified.

If we were to judge Ludwell by the pattern of slave ownership revealed in the tax records of the 1780's, he would belong very nearly at the middle of the hundred leading families of the colony. These tax records, which have been most effectively analyzed by Professor Jackson T. Main, furnish the only comprehensive records on how widely slave ownership was distributed in Virginia before the nineteenth century. While the position of the leading families had begun to decline somewhat by the 1780's, the change was as yet so slight that the statistics are generally reliable for the entire later colonial period.

What becomes immediately clear from these tax records is the error of regarding even most of the wealthiest planters as having owned "hundreds" of Negroes. One man, Charles Carter, owned 785. He was followed in turn by William Allen with 700, Robert Beverly of Essex County with 592, Robert Carter of Nomini Hall with 445, and David Ross, the Richmond merchant-planter, with 400. Aside from these top five there were only eighteen other men in the entire colony who owned more than 200 slaves. The average for the hundred leading families was about 180 slaves, eighty on the home plantation and about a hundred elsewhere. A number of families who fell within this top group owned far less than a hundred Negroes.

If there were relatively few large-scale slaveholders in Virginia, the vast majority of families in the average Tidewater or Piedmont county nonetheless owned at least a small number of Negroes. In a sampling of eight of these counties the records indicated that three-fourths of the heads of families held slaves. Forty per cent of them, however, owned fewer than five Negroes. In the light of these statistics a true picture of slavery in colonial Virginia must take into account the humbler man who owned no more than two or three slaves as well as the more substantial planter.

Until the rationale of the American Revolution had begun to work its logic on the minds of Virginians, any doubt which the average colonist ever had about the wisdom of slavery stemmed either from the unpleasant prospect that the slaves would one day rise up and butcher the master class or else from suspicion that, as a business proposition, slavery simply did not pay its way. The threat of insurrection was in part dealt with through the tightening of the black codes, as well as by the attempt to discourage new importations of Negroes; but it was less easy to deal so directly with the economics of slavery.

The relative advantages and disadvantages of slave labor was, however, a subject often on the mind of the planter. Philip Fithian's account of a conversation with the wife of Robert Carter adequately sums up the reaction in theory of many planters to a situation with which they were unable to deal in fact:

After Supper I had a long conversation with Mrs Carter concerning Negroes in Virginia, & find that She esteems their value at no higher rate than I do. We both concluded, (& I am pretty certain that the conclusion is just) that if in Mr Carters, or in any Gentleman Estate, all the Negroes should be sold, & the Money put to Interest in safe hands, & let the Lands which these Negroes now work lie wholly uncultivated, the bare Interest of the Price of the Negroes would be a much greater yearly income than what is now received from their working the Lands, making no allowance at all for the trouble & Risk of the Masters as to the Crops, & Negroes.— How much greater then must be the value of an Estate here if these poor enslaved Africans were all in their native desired Country, & in their Room industrious Tenants, who being born in freedom, by a laudable care, would not only inrich their Landlords, but would raise a hardy Offspring to be the Strength & honour of the Colony.

One reason the planters questioned the profit in slave labor was the high cost of investment in slaves. In more pessimistic moments they also criticized their Negroes as wasteful and unproductive workers, either from lack of skill or deliberate resistance to forced labor.

To a large degree, the planters were inclined to rationalize other deficiencies in the agricultural methods of the colony at the expense of their Negroes. If there was one way in which slavery succeeded, it was as an economic system. Any problems of debt or credit arising from large investment in slaves was in reality a by-product of the uncertainties of tobacco cultivation. The supposed inefficiency and ineptitude of slave labor was more likely to be the fault of the wasteful methods of farming common to almost everyone who tilled the Virginia soil. Moreover, the cheapness of a slave's maintenance easily outweighed high purchase price, lack of training or skill, and even the prospect of his unproductive old age.

Whatever doubts the Virginia planter may have felt about the wisdom of enslaving an alien people, it must have seemed in the mid-eighteenth century that slavery was certainly here to stay. The rapid growth of the Negro population, the size of the slaveowners' investment, the usefulness of the labor, and outright fear combined to make the replacement of slavery unthinkable.

COLONIAL BLACK CODES

The evolution of the Negro's legal status from ordinary indentured servant to servant for life to slave was followed by the development of a separate legal code, distinct trial procedures, and harsher punishments for Negroes accused of criminal acts. Inevitably the slave's lack of personal freedom would have necessitated some revision in the English legal system that had been transported to Virginia. But it was unrelenting fear of the Negro as a potential insurrectionist and constant determination to police his conduct rigidly that instigated most of the early laws affecting Negro slaves.

Only in the last two decades of the seventeenth century did anything more than the faintest beginning·of a separate criminal law for Negroes begin to appear. An act of 1680 for preventing Negro insurrections was the first real "black code" in Virginia, providing specific punishments for the three crimes of leaving the master's property without permission; lifting a hand against a "Christian," that is, a white man; and for hiding or resisting capture after running away. Conviction on the last charge required the death penalty. A 1691 statute that was of the greatest importance as the first legal restriction on manumission of slaves in Virginia also provided a systematic plan for raising a force of men to recapture "outlying slaves," or runaways who were in hiding. Then in 1692 the legislature provided the first trial procedures, in particular the denial of jury trial, which applied specifically to Negro slaves.

There were three more or less comprehensive pieces of legislation in the eighteenth century covering the trial, punishment, and regulation of slaves. The first passed in 1705 to be replaced in 1723 by one which was in turn superseded by the act of 1748. These were the basic codes for the later colonial period, and most of the other legislation affecting Negro crimes, with the exception of laws dealing with runaways, was not much more than a minor modification of these two measures.

As has already been suggested, the first law aimed at a crime by Negroes other than running away was the 1680 statute designed to prevent insurrections by punishing slaves who kept their master's property without permission or resisted a white man in any way. On the supposition that this act went unnoticed

the Assembly required two years later that it be read twice a year in every church. The more comprehensive statute of 1723 sought new safeguards against an armed rising by withdrawing the privilege of benefit of clergy from Negroes convicted of plotting or attempting such rebellion and by forbidding all assemblies of slaves that were not licensed by the masters and held for public worship. It also denied all Negroes free or slave the right to possess weapons, except that free Negroes who were householders or militiamen might keep a single gun and Negroes residing on the frontier might be licensed by the justice of the peace to carry arms. All of these restrictions continued in force under the law of 1748.

Most crimes other than running away or rising in rebellion that a Negro might commit were actions defined in laws that applied equally to all persons in the colony. It is revealing, however, that two felonies, hog stealing and the administration of poisonous medicines, were the occasion of special provisions dealing exclusively with slaves. Hog stealing reached the point that on the third conviction it became a capital offense without benefit of clergy. Such were the risks involved in the temptations of the delicate flavor of roast pig.

The restriction of poisonous medicines obviously arose out of the belief of the whites that a great many Negroes continued to practice the witchcraft and tribal medicine they had brought from Africa both in honest, if primitive, attempts to cure ailing slaves but also in malicious attempts to destroy an enemy. One section of the 1748 code provided capital punishment for Negroes who prepared and administered medicine of any sort, unless their owner had consented. Benefit of clergy was allowable only where the slave could prove there had been no evil intent. In the wave of Negro crimes which David Mays described in Caroline County from 1761–1764 there were no less than three trials under this law in a three months period during 1762 with convictions in two of them.

Beginning with the legislation of

1692 a separate court procedure developed for the trial of Negroes differing markedly in its rapid movement to trial and lack of constitutional guarantees from that accorded the free man. In capital cases the core of this process was (1) the immediate imprisonment of the slave, (2) issuance by the governor of a commission of oyer and terminer* to persons in the county involved to arraign and indict the offender and to take for evidence the confession of the accused or the oaths of two witnesses, or one in some cases, and (3) "without the sollemnitie of jury" to pass such judgment as the law allowed. Throughout the colonial era there was but one modification in this method of trial. In 1765 the governor was permitted to issue general commissions of oyer and terminer to four or more justices of the peace in each county, including one of the quorum, thereby eliminating the necessity of a special commission for each trial.

Initially the procedure for trying slaves did not provide for testimony by other Negroes. In 1723, however, it became permissible in capital cases involving Negroes to take such testimony from Negroes, Indians, or mulattoes "as shall seem convincing," wording which clearly implied that they were not to be accepted as sworn witnesses nor to be questioned at all, except when absolutely necessary. However, this provision for the use of slave testimony in 1723 may have been an opening wedge for employing Negro witnesses far more widely than the law intended. For a new law of 1732 stated that no Negro, mulatto, or Indian should be admitted in court, be sworn as a witness, or give evidence in a case—practices which the law complained had been allowed, even in the General Court—except in the trial of a slave for a capital offense. One subsequent modification occurred in 1748 when free Christian Negroes, Indians, and mulattoes were allowed to appear in any case involving another Negro, Indian, or mulatto. In brief, however,

all these technicalities come down to the fact that the slaves normally could testify only in a capital case involving another Negro.

After 1732 the Negro possessed some fragments of that medieval remnant, benefit of clergy, to soften the harsh processes of justice under which he was often tried and convicted. This is not the place for a discussion of the long evolution of that institution from its origin as a means of protecting persons in clerical orders from trial in civil courts to the point that it saved all literate persons and finally virtually the entire population from certain punishments. To the Virginia Negro it was a means of escaping the prescribed punishment for his first commission of a good many capital crimes. If his felony fell within benefit of clergy, the slave was burned in the hand to show that he had exhausted his use of the privilege. Then he received corporal punishment and was released.

There is some question as to how early in the history of Virginia Negro slaves were able to claim benefit of clergy. Dalzell's study regards the 1732 law regulating the pleading of this privilege by Negroes as both the first regulation of benefit of clergy in the laws of the colony and the first occasion of its extension to slaves. However, there was an earlier law in 1723 which placed insurrection or murder by a slave outside the privileges of benefit of clergy, an indication that Negroes might already have been clergyable.

But Dalzell was probably entirely correct in thinking there was a considerable area of doubt about how far benefit of clergy extended to Negro slaves, and even to other Virginians. In particular the laws of England had not allowed women and persons who were illiterate to claim benefit of clergy until the reigns of William and Mary and Anne. It was not at all certain that these acts applied in the colonies to anyone. Moreover, the laws affecting the baptism of Negroes had not considered the possibility that conversion to Christianity conferred the right to benefit of clergy on slaves.

The 1732 legislation was the direct outgrowth of a case involving a Negro

* "Oyer and terminer" means literally "to hear and determine"; it refers to an open hearing or examination.

slave in which many of these doubts were combined. Mary Aggie, Virginia-born, Christianized, and the property of a Williamsburg widow, had committed a larceny for which she would have been clergyable in England, if a free woman. Governor Gooch interested himself in the case for some unexplained reason and after Mary Aggie's conviction by the Commission of Oyer and Terminer for York County, had an application for benefit of clergy entered in her behalf. The case was eventually considered by the Council and the General Court, and then submitted to England for a ruling. At that point all evidence of the outcome disappears, but then in 1732 the Virginia Assembly passed laws affecting benefit of clergy for women, illiterates, and slaves.

Further definitions of benefit of clergy for slaves usually took the form of placing certain felonies outside the plea of clergy. Insurrection or murder fell beyond its scope in 1723. Manslaughter, felonious breaking and entering, and thefts involving more than five shillings were exempted in 1732. Then it was denied for a third conviction for hog stealing and for the malicious administration of poisonous medicines by the laws of 1748. So, in effect, so far as slaves were concerned the privilege of benefit of clergy began gradually to contract, except that in 1772 there was one redefinition of its applicability in cases of breaking and entering that favored the accused.

Cases in which a Negro was on trial for a felony usually came to the courts with a minimum of delay. The special commissions of oyer and terminer helped speed the process, but efficiency was less at issue than the desire to impress other Negroes with the swift course of justice. In the long run a speedy trial was in the Negro's best interest, for slaves who did languish in jail awaiting trial sometimes paid a heavy penalty in physical suffering before they could begin to pay for their crime. In its 1762 session, for instance, the Burgesses noted an allowance of £3:15:0 to a Caroline County man to compensate him for loss of thirty days labor by a slave who

had been frostbitten while confined. That same session it had to allow £80 to the owner of a slave who had lost both his legs and finally died from the frostbite he suffered in a cold jail.

Peter Hansborough of Stafford County petitioned the Burgesses in an even worse case in 1771, but the delegates did not seem much disposed to compensate Hansborough for the death of his slave Sharper. The Negro had been charged with administering medicine illegally and was imprisoned to await examination by the justices. The weather turned so cold and rainy that, while Hansborough made his appearance at court, the justices declined to attend. Hansborough inquired after his slave and "found he was bitt by the Frost to Such a Degree that it Commanded Pity from every human heart." This was December, and the trial dragged on until May, when Sharper was acquitted. Hansborough related that he then "took the Poor distressed Slave home . . . [where he] . . . died."

Just as the very nature of slave status had demanded trial procedures that to some extent abridged the traditional English and colonial guarantees of individual right, it just as logically required a system of punishment that was exclusively corporal. The courts might fine a master whose neglect contributed in some way to a criminal act of one of his Negroes, but the slave could not normally make satisfaction in this way. For minor offenses or when the slave was able to avail himself of benefit of clergy, whipping became the prescribed penalty —10 lashes for coming on a plantation without permission, 39 lashes for attending an unlawful meeting, or 39 for possessing weapons illegally, to cite a few examples.

More serious crimes which did not warrant capital punishment, even in the harsh criminal codes of the day, required what may have been a more unpleasant fate than death itself. That penalty was mutilation or dismemberment. A slave giving false evidence would, for instance, receive his 39 lashes and then have his ears nailed to the pillory for half an hour, after which they would be cut off. Under the law of 1748 his ears would have been nailed to the pillory and then cut off one at a time rather than simultaneously. Dismemberment was a favorite punishment for the slave who continually ran away, went abroad at night, or lay in hiding. Both the 1723 and 1748 acts specify its use for these offenses. Since the dismemberment usually took the form of cutting off a foot, it was a practical, if cruel, way of curbing the sort of ungovernable Negro who really constituted the greatest threat of all against slavery as a police institution. That dismemberment sometimes reached proportions which struck even slaveowners as barbarous is, however, evidenced by a 1769 statute which in the future forbade the castration of a slave for continually lying out and reserved that punishment solely for Negroes guilty of the attempted rape of a white woman.

Finally there were the whole series of crimes for which conviction carried the death penalty, the felonies for which white persons would also have been executed plus offenses such as rebellion or the administering of medicines that applied only to slaves. According to the customary practice of colonial Virginia slaves were ordinarily hanged, but a slave named Eve who was convicted in Orange County of poisoning her master was drawn upon a hurdle to the place of execution and there burned at the stake. Then there are also instances in which the head of a slave who had been hanged was cut off and put on public exhibition.

One economic problem arose with capital punishment of a slave. The owner was apt to view the execution as costing him the loss of a valuable piece of property, no matter how serious the slave's crime had been. In the 1705 statute affecting trial procedure for capital offenses, the justices were impowered to put a reasonable valuation upon any slave they condemned. When this valuation had been certified to the Assembly, the owner would be reimbursed from public funds. This method of compensation remained in force throughout the colonial period with the result that few sessions of the Assembly fail to record favorable action on the request of some owner to be paid for an executed slave.

The punishment which the courts meted out to slaves for crimes against public order in no way interfered with the disciplining of slaves by their owners and overseers. In fact, the law protected to extreme limits the master's privilege of punishing his slaves. One of the earliest pieces of legislation affecting slavery was the 1669 statute exempting a master from indictment for felony if a slave were killed while under punishment. The law reasoned that there could be no felony without malicious intent and that no one could be presumed to destroy his own property deliberately and maliciously. The Assembly made some dent in this line of reasoning in 1723, by providing that the master might be indicted if there were at least one lawful witness to testify that the killing of the slave had been a willful act. But with this one unlikely exception owners remained exempt from prosecution for the death of a slave under correction, even though new royal governors were often instructed to work for laws to punish masters who deliberately killed or maimed a slave.

The dissection of a long list of laws is a tedious business at best; and once their contents have been outlined, there is not much more to be said. One significant development in the eighteenth century, however, was the collection of most of the criminal law affecting Negroes into the two comprehensive statutes of 1723 and 1748. They provided the colony with a "black code" nearly as well-defined and systematic as those of a later day.

This much can be said for the justice administered under these laws—it was often harsh, but it was uniform and not arbitrary. And it was rapid, for the slave did not often languish in jail awaiting trial. To that extent the slaves of colonial Virginia could have fared worse, as indeed they did in parts of the New World.

The net effect of these statutes, however, was to make the law for the Negro slave almost exclusively a police instrument for maintaining the stability of society and largely to demolish that more attractive side of law, the safeguarding of the individual from unnecessary invasions of his person. Perhaps only the uncomfortable fact that the slave was not fully a person in the eyes of the law saved this one-sidedness from seriously damaging, for free men even, the traditional guarantees to the individual that Virginia had inherited from English law.

Herbert S. Klein

THE NEGRO AND THE CHURCH OF ENGLAND IN VIRGINIA

This excerpt from Professor Klein's comparison of slavery in Cuba and Virginia points out some of the difficulties involved in developing chattel slavery in a Christian society. Nevertheless, despite these difficulties, slavery proved to be compatible with Virginia Anglicanism, as well as with Latin American Catholicism. But Klein believes that religion in Virginia exercised little influence in forming the characteristics of slavery, in contrast to Latin America, where it had a significant effect. Instead it appears that slavery was a prime factor in shaping other Virginia social institutions. Professor Klein, a Latin America specialist, teaches at the University of Chicago.

NOT only was the church after the Restoration terribly concerned about the religion of the white colonists, but it also began to take an increasingly involved position on the status of the Negro and Indian heathens within England's American Empire. This concern with the plight of the Negro slave, especially, is heavily attested to by the growing movement among the lower and upper clergy for conversion, education, and even emancipation. This movement began as early as the end of the seventeenth century, and one of its first advocates was Morgan Godwyn, the angry clergyman who served in the British West Indies and in the colony of Virginia, and whose *The Negro's and Indians Advocate* (1680) created a good deal of sentiment. This growing awareness of the complete lack of impact of the church on the Negro slaves, in sharp contrast to that of the Catholic church in the Spanish and French islands, as many Church of England men noted, caused the Bishop of London to put pressure on the crown.

In the royal instructions to Governor Culpeper of Virginia in 1681–82, the crown proposed that:

Ye shall endeavour to get a Law passed for the restraining of any inhuman severity which by ill masters or overseers may be used towards their Christian Servants or Slaves. And you are alsoe with the assistance of the Council and Assembly, to find out the best means to facilitate and encourage the conversion of Negroes to the Christian Religion, *wherein you are to leave a due* caution and regards to ye property of the Inhabitants and safety of the Colonies.

The unusual restraint of this request indicates the royal government's recognition of the primacy of local law and custom over the humanitarian demands of the clergymen.

Nevertheless, despite the inaction of the local colonial governments, the English hierarchy was becoming deeply con-

Reprinted from *Slavery in the Americas* by Herbert S. Klein by permission of The University of Chicago Press, pp. 113–116, 119–125. Copyright 1967 by the University of Chicago.

cerned over the failure of the colonials to Christianize the Negro slaves. Finding that little could be accomplished directly through regular church and governmental channels, the bishops decided that the only alternative was a missionary society, completely financed from England. Thus, in 1701, the hierarchy in England founded the famous Society for the Propagation of the Gospel in Foreign Parts (SPG).

That one of the primary aims of the society was conversion of the slaves was understood by the bishops from the very beginning. Thus in the annual sermon given to the society in 1710, Bishop William Fleetwood bitterly attacked the masters of slaves who refused to permit their conversion to Christianity. He claimed the refusal to permit baptism and Christian education was:

A thing so common in all our *Plantations* abroad, that I have reason to doubt, whether there be any Exception of any People of *ours,* who cause their slaves to be Baptized. What do these people think of Christ? . . . That He who came from Heaven, to purchase to Himself a Church, with his own precious Blood, should sit contented, and behold with unconcern, those who profess themselves his Servants, excluding from its Gates those who would gladly enter if they might, and exercising no less Cruelty to their Souls (as far as they are able) than to their Bodies?

These People were made to be as Happy as themselves, and are as capable of being so; and however hard their Condition be in this World, with respect to their Captivity and Subjugation. . . . They were bought with the same Price, purchased with the same Blood of Christ, their common Saviour and Redeemer; and in order to all this, they were to have the Means of Salvation put into their Hands, they were to be instructed in the Faith of *Christ,* to have the Terms and Conditions fairly offered to them.

Not only did Bishop Fleetwood attack the very Christianity of the masters, but also considered that this was probably their greatest sin, for he declared, "no Man living can assign a better and more justifiable Cause, for God's with-holding Mercy from a *Christian,* than that *Christian's* with-holding the Mercy of *Christianity* from an Unbeliever." The radical

bishop even went so far as to attack slavery itself, holding, as Adam Smith was later to proclaim, that hired labor was the far superior system of labor and that slavery should be abolished. He attacked the ideas of the colonists, which held that Christianity challenged the slave status, but instead of proclaiming the docility of slaves under Christian doctrine as some clerics did, he properly attacked the Christinity of the colonists who would refuse to treat fellow human beings with Christian brotherly love. Finally, he proposed that the society take up the crucial task of Christianizing the infidels, Negroes and slaves, and that this example would have a powerful impact on the masters, who apparently were unimpressed by "the Example both of *French* and *Spaniards* . . . , who all along have brought their Slaves to Baptism."

This call appears to have been heeded, for in the annual sermon of 1740, Bishop Secker pointed to the work of the society in this special area. But the bishop noted the vast difficulty still faced by the church in this work, as only a few slaves had been converted and thousands yet remained outside the fold.

For it is not to be expected, that Masters, too commonly negligent of Christianity themselves, will take much Pains to teach it to their Slaves: whom even the better Part of them are in a great measure habituated to consider, as they do their Cattle, merely with a View to the Profit arising from them. Not a few therefore have openly opposed their Instruction, from an Imagination, now indeed proved and acknowledged to be groundless, that Baptism would entitle them to Freedom. . . . And some, it may be feared, have been averse to their becoming Christians, because, after that, no Pretence will remain for not treating them like Men.

By the middle of the eighteenth century, both within and without the society, the upper clergy was beginning to put pressure on the colonies to change their local customs and laws on these subjects and to create a new panoply of beliefs that would permit the church to carry on the work of conversion in a positive atmosphere.

The Bishop of London in 1742 put

great pressure on Commissary Blair to indicate to the local government his great zeal in converting Negroes to the Christian faith and to get that government to support a school for Negroes. But incapable of even fully protecting standard dogma and church practice, Blair and his successors could accomplish little. As for the SPG, the demands on its resources were so great that it concentrated its efforts in the British West Indies, where the bulk of the New World slaves resided, and in the colonies in which the church was not yet established.

This meant, in essence, that whatever might be the feelings of the hierarchy in England about the desirability of conversion of the slaves to Christianity and their participation in the sacraments, this desire had little, if any, impact on New World conditions. With no clergymen capable of opposing these assumptions and customs, the planters felt under no obligation to change their ways. Thus the religious life of the slave was wholly dependent upon the will of his master, and this was determined almost exclusively by local custom.

Unfortunately for the Negro slave, custom was indifferent, if not openly hostile, to the conversion of Negro slaves. In the early years of the seventeenth century, there had existed the almost universal belief that conversion for the slave required his freedom, since Christians could not hold other Christians in bondage. But although the General Assembly eventually declared that this was not so, the idea was hard to uproot, and it persisted throughout the colonial period. Even when this factor was resolved or admitted by the reluctant master, there was still the key fear of education making the slaves intractable. As the Reverend Hugh Jones reported, he constantly tried to assuage this fear among colonials:

As for baptizing Indians and Negroes, several of the people disapprove of it, because they say it often makes them proud, and not so good servants: But these, and such objections, are easily refuted, for Christianity encourages and orders them to become more humble and better servants, and not worse, than when they were heathens.

He did agree with the general opinion, however, that held that Negro slaves should not be taught to read and write, since this "has been found to be dangerous upon several political accounts, especially self-preservation."

Although there could be found masters who sponsored the baptism of their slaves and encouraged them to learn the catechism, and some who even read to them from the Bible, these were usually the exception rather than the rule. The pattern, in fact, was quite haphazard, and in the majority of cases conversion was never properly undertaken.

* * *

The Reverend John Brunskill of Wilmington Parish probably best summed up the problem when he concluded that:

The Negroes who are slaves to the whites cannot, I think, be said to be of any Religion for as there is no law of the Colony oblidging their Masters or Owners to instruct them in the principles of Christianity and so they are hardly to be persuaded by the Minister to take so much pains with them, by which means the poor creatures generally live and die without it.

Even for the minority that were baptized, coverted, and taught the Christian religion, there were no positive rewards. No matter how Christian, no master allowed his slaves to be married. For if the sacrament of marriage was not to be made a totally ridiculous right, then Negro slaves could not be admitted. For by this admission, it was recognized that human agencies had no right to separate the conjugal couple, and this was never accepted. For even when the best of masters died, the constant fluidity of fortunes meant that no slave community could remain intact beyond a few generations, and families were simply not sold together. This was uneconomical and therefore impractical. As the Virginia baptist chronicler John Leland noted in 1790, "the marriage of slaves, is a subject not known in our code of laws. What promises soever they make, their masters may and do part them at pleasure."

As for the complex web of social organizations to which the Cuban slave had recourse, this simply did not exist under the established church of Virginia. There were no fraternal brotherhoods, no great processionals and special holidays, and absolutely no syncretism of Christian belief with the folk religion of African origin. After 1740, there did exist, for the Negro slaves on the frontier of Virginia, the possibility of being admitted into the mass evangelical movement that was known as the Great Awakening. From 1740 and especially after 1760, numbers of Methodist, Baptist, Presbyterian, and a host of other sect preachers began invading the frontier counties of Virginia above the tidewater. Most of these preachers, like Wesley himself, were bitter opponents of slavery and welcomed the Negroes into the church. Thus John Leland in his Virginia Chronicle of 1790 reported:

The poor slaves, under all their hardships, discover as great inclination for religion as the free-born do, when they engage in the service of God, they spare no pains. It is nothing strange for them to walk 20 miles on Sunday morning to meeting, and back again at night. They are remarkable for learning a toon soon, and have very melodious voices.

They cannot read, and therefore are more exposed to delusion than the whites are; but many of them give clear, rational accounts of a work of grace in their harts, and evidence of the same by their lives. When religion is lively they are remarkable fond of meeting together, to sing, pray and exhort, and sometimes preach, and seem to be unwearied in the procession. They seem in general to put more confidence in their own colour, then they do in whites; when they attempt to preach, they seldom fail of being very zealous; their language is broken, but they understand each other, and the whites may gain their ideas. A few of them have undertaken to administer baptism, but it generally ends in confusion; they commonly are more noisy in time of preaching than the whites, and are more subject to bodily exercise, and if they meet with any encouragement in these things, they grow extravagant.

But these camp meetings and nonhierarchical churches were not open for the majority of Virginia Negroes, who continued to reside in the areas dominated by the Church of England. Nor were the masters too ready to permit them the openness of these great revivalist gatherings. As Leland himself notes: ". . . many masters and overseers will whip and torture the poor creatures for going to meeting, even at night, when the labor of the day is done." As fear of insurrection developed in the period after independence, such church meetings became less and less common as public gatherings of slaves, even for religious purposes, were severely restricted. Even the evangelical churches themselves, after a brief period of strong support for Negro conversion and religious instruction, by the early decades of the nineteenth century had conformed to planter opinion and had kept slave conversion and participation to a minimum. They had even gone so far as to develop a special system of "religion without letters" for the special evangelization of free Negroes as well as slave. When, in 1802, the Baptist church discovered that because of its leadership in the conversion movement it had the startling number of 9,000 colored communicants—mostly slaves, it decided to check the potential power of this group by ruling that only free persons could exercise authority within the Church. By the time of the famous 1804 and 1805 laws on religious meetings of slaves, it became virtually impossible for the slave to participate freely in the revivalist meetings of the evangelical churches, and his role in these churches quickly declined to the same point as his role in the Anglican church and its successor.

Not only were these churches incapable of undertaking a general conversion of the slaves, but they were also unable to promote manumission. The common pattern of manumission inspired by the church, which was the accepted custom and practice in Cuba, was unknown in Protestant Virginia. Although the Methodists and Quakers early demanded that their members give up slave trading and emancipate their slaves, and although several revolutionary leaders followed Enlightenment thought to its logical conclusion and freed their Negroes, no powerful undercurrent of emancipation ever occurred. Quaker emancipations were few and of little consequence, and the Methodist leadership was soon forced to condone the existence of slave-holding even among its traveling clergy and to give up its proposals for emancipation. The Anglican hierarchy also developed a powerful commitment to emancipation at the end of the eighteenth century, but it took forceful Parliamentary legislation to carry out emancipation even in the West Indies. But in Virginia this emancipation movement was never reflected in the local episcopal hierarchy, when the latter was finally established in 1790.

Unlike the clergy of Cuba, the clergy of Virginia was unable to convince the planters that emancipation was a good act in the sight of God and was to be considered a common and accepted form of pious action. Nor, on the other hand, could the morally aroused and committed clergy, of whatever denomination, convince the masters that slavery was essentially a moral evil and that on these grounds the slaves should be emancipated as expeditiously as possible. Since emancipation could not be forced on moral grounds from above, nor could it become a part of routine common practice from below, the whole emancipation movement in Virginia was at best a haphazard and distinctly minor affair. In fact, from the late seventeenth to the late eighteenth century, emancipation was for all intents and purposes outlawed by the state. Even when private emancipation was again permitted after 1782, the free colored were only a small part of the colored class, representing at the time of the first federal census in 1790 only 4% of the total colored population. Nor was any major change indicated in the half-century between the first federal census and the Civil War. While the percentage of freedmen slowly rose from decade to decade, it only reached 11% in 1860. With roughly the same number of colored, in both Cuba and Virginia in 1860–61, Virginia had only 58,042 freedmen (or 11% of the total colored) to Cuba's 213,167 (or 35%).

As for the development of formal education for the free Negroes, this was informal and haphazard in the extreme, except for one short-lived experiment. In the late 1720's, Dr. Thomas Bray, who had been commissary in Maryland for the Bishop of London, helped found a group of missionaries known as Bray's Associates who directed considerable attention to founding schools for Negroes in the American colonies. A leading founder of the SPG, Bray received a private donation of £900 to found several schools in the North American colonies. After setting up such a successful school with the aid of Benjamin Franklin in Philadelphia in 1759, Bray helped establish a Negro school in Williamsburg in 1764. Under the direction of Commissary Dawson, local clerics, and Mrs. Ann Wager, the school soon opened its doors to twenty-four Negro students and made progress in the area. It appears to have won some local support, for a local printer, Mr. William Hunter, left in his will in 1761 some £7 for the support of Mrs. Wager. But despite the initial success and support granted to the school, with the death of Mrs. Wager in 1774 the school ceased to operate. In fact, in the agitation of those years, all the Negro and Indian schools on the North American continent founded by Bray and his associates, as well as by the SPG, also collapsed. The Williamsburg school was also the model for a school in Fredericksburg that lasted five years in the 1770's, but with the American Revolution the source of English enthusiasm and funds for these schools was destroyed, and local planter interest seems to have been exhausted. It appears that aside from these schools, neither free nor slave Negroes were permitted regular education by the local county schools.

There was some attempt by the vestries, however, to provide for the free Negroes, orphans, and poor some type of apprenticeship in which they were also taught to read and write by the person to whom they were indentured. The vestry of Petsworth Parish in 1716, for example, required that for his indenture, Mr. Ralph Bevis was to

give George Petsworth, a mulattoe boy of the age of 2 years, 3 years' schooling, and carefully to Instruct him afterwards that he may read well in any part of the Bible, also to instruct and Learn him ye s[ai]d mulattoe boy such Lawful way and ways that he may be able after his Indented time expired to gitt his own Liveing, and to allow him suficient meat, Drink, washing, and apparill, until the expiration of ye sd time &c. . . .

But these indenture and apprenticeship programs were for only a few free Negroes, and aside from the temporary Negro school experiment on the eve of the American Revolution, there seems to have been almost no serious effort, or no successful one, by the church to educate the Virginia Negro. No Negro was admitted to William and Mary College, and none appears to have been trained by the church in local parish schools for the liberal professions, as in Cuba; and in the harsh reaction that took place by the early nineteenth century, even basic literacy was denied the freedmen.

Thus the Virginia church, dominated by the planter elite, offered no educational escape opportunities for the free Negroes, and none whatsoever for the slaves. It totally denied the right to slave marriages, and by and large in the colonial period did not even Christianize the majority of African Negroes: Finally, the Virginia established church provided no social appenditures that could enrich the community life of the Negroes. Under Anglicanism there was no religious brotherhood system, no great pageantry and processions, and no folk religious syncretism, which was such an important part of the fabric of Catholic Cuba. Although after 1740 the dissenter groups in the Great Awakening provided some types of compensation in the evangelical and revivalist meetings, which gave birth to the future Negro church movement, this activity was confined to the frontier in the colonial period and involved only a few thousand Negro slaves. For the Great Awakening in colonial Virginia was the work of only a handful of ministers, and it never penetrated into the Tidewater parishes where the overwhelming majority of slaves lived under Anglican masters. Even with the breakdown of the established church in the 1780's and the tremendous growth of permanent Methodist, Baptist, and Presbyterian church movements, the slaves in the plantation areas still found themselves under the domination of Episcopalians. And by the 1840's, the great rendering of the evangelical churches into northern and southern branches assured the planter's domination of Church attitudes toward the Negro by all sects except the Quakers.

Thus despite the greater religious diversity of Virginia in the nineteenth century, the customs and practices established under the Anglican church of colonial Virginia persisted. And in the nineteenth century, as in the two preceding centuries of Anglican control, the law remained glaringly silent on the religious rights and needs of the African slave.

Leon F. Litwack

SLAVERY TO FREEDOM

In the following excerpt from *North of Slavery: The Negro in the Free States, 1790–1860,* Professor Litwack describes the pattern of emancipation and abolition which swept the Northern states in the Revolutionary era. This movement against slavery illustrates the real, if limited, impact of Revolutionary ideology on a long-established social institution. Yet, even though slavery was abolished in the North, the racial attitudes which were part of it persisted; while in the South, abolition sentiment faltered, unable to match the pressure generated for the perpetuation of such a broadly based social and economic system. As a result, although Northern emancipation made slavery an exclusively Southern phenomenon, most Americans continued to believe in White superiority and Black inferiority. Professor Litwack teaches at the University of California, Berkeley.

O N the eve of the War of Independence, American Negro slavery knew no sectional boundaries. Every colony recognized it and sharply defined the legal position of free and enslaved blacks. The Declaration of Independence boldly asserted the natural rights of man but made no mention of slavery; the Constitution subsequently sanctioned and protected the institution without naming it. By that time, however, the Revolution had worked some important changes. Human bondage, it seemed certain, would henceforth assume a sectional character, for the North had sentenced it to a slow death. By 1800, some 36,505 northern Negroes still remained in bondage, most of them in New York and New Jersey, but almost every northern state had either abolished slavery outright or had provided for its gradual extinction.*

* Slavery was abolished by the constitutions of Vermont (1777), Ohio (1802), Illinois (1818), and Indiana (1816); by a judicial decision in Massachusetts (1783); by constitutional interpretation in New Hampshire; and by gradual-abolition acts in Pennsylvania (1780), Rhode Island (1784), Connecticut (1784 and 1797), New York (1799 and 1817), and New Jersey (1804).

State statutes, constitutions, and court decisions recorded the methods of northern abolition but said little about the motives. Why did northern slaveholders surrender, with little apparent opposition or compensation, a valuable investment in human property? Perhaps, some have argued, it was not that valuable. In the complex economy and uncongenial climate of the North, slave labor presumably proved to be unprofitable; savage Africans lacked the mental capacity to learn anything more than how to tend a single crop. Climate and geography thus prompted the employing class to turn to the more profitable use of free white laborers, thereby dooming slavery. "The winter here was always unfavourable to the African constitution," one New Englander explained. "For this reason, white labourers were preferable to blacks."

Although commonly accepted, the economic explanation for northern abolition has not been adequately demonstrated. Plantation capitalism did not root itself in the North; the economy of that region came to be based largely on commerce, manufacturing, and small-

scale agriculture. But this did not necessarily preclude the profitable use of slave
labor. On the contrary, evidence suggests
that the scarcity and expense of free
white labor prompted ambitious northerners to make a profitable use of slaves
and that these Negro bondsmen could
and did perform successfully a variety
of tasks—agricultural and mechanical,
skilled and unskilled—in a diversified
economy. On farms, slaves assisted in
the production of foodstuffs and dairy
products and in sheep and stock raising;
in the cities, they worked in various
skilled trades—as bakers, carpenters,
cabinetmakers, sawyers, blacksmiths,
printers, tailors, and coopers—and perhaps most prominently in the maritime
industry.

Wherever utilized, slave labor was
still cheap labor. Free labor, on the other
hand, involved additional expense. In
comparing the economic value of the
two groups, John Adams admitted that
his personal abhorrence of slavery had
cost him "thousands of dollars for the
labor and subsistence of free men, which
I might have saved by the purchase of
Negroes at times when they were very
cheap." Moreover, some northern slaveholders appeared unconvinced that abolition would rid them of an economic
encumbrance. Vigorously opposing a
proposed duty on the importation of
Negroes, a group of Pennsylvania merchants cited the scarcity of laborers and
artisans and argued that additional
slaves would reduce "the exorbitant
price of Labour, and, in all probability,
bring our Staple Commoditys to their
usual prices." Despite public abolition
sentiment, a Massachusetts physician
recalled in 1795, it took legal action to
force many slaveholders to part with
their human chattel. Such reluctance
would seem to suggest that slaves at
least performed some useful and profitable services.

If slave labor was indeed unprofitable,
not only did some masters reluctantly
give up their property, but white workers
protested often and bitterly against the
Negro's competitive position. By the end
of the seventeenth century, for example,
workers in New York City had already

complained that Negro labor had "soe
much impoverisht them, that they Cannot by their Labours gett a Competency
for the Maintenance of themselves and
Family's." In 1737, the lieutenant governor of New York asked the Assembly
to consider the justifiable complaints of
"honest and industrious tradesmen" that
skilled slave labor had reduced them to
unemployment and poverty. Twenty
years later, when Lieutenant Governor
James Delancey proposed a poll tax on
slaves, he argued that this would attract
more white laborers and occasion little
local resistance. "[T]he price of labor is
now become so high," he explained, "and
hence the owners of slaves reap such
advantage, that they cannot reasonably
complain of a tax on them." In Massachusetts, John Adams recalled, the opposition of white labor assured the extinction of slavery, for it "would no longer
suffer the rich to employ these sable
rivals so much to their injury." Had
slavery not been abolished, Adams observed, the white laborers would simply
have removed the Negro by force. In any
case, their hostility had already rendered
the institution unprofitable. "Their
scoffs and insults, their continual insin-
uations, filled the negroes with discontent, made them lazy, idle, proud, vicious, and at length wholly useless to
their masters, to such a degree that the
abolition of slavery became a measure
of economy."

If contemporary explanations have
any validity, the liquidation of slavery
in the North should not be considered
simply on the grounds of profits and
losses, climate, or geography. Abolition
sentiment generally ignored these factors and chose instead to emphasize one
particular theme: that the same principles used to justify the American Revolution, particularly John Locke's natural-rights philosophy, also condemned
and doomed Negro slavery. Such an institution could not be reconciled with
colonial efforts to resist English tyranny;
indeed, its existence embarrassed the
American cause. "To contend for liberty," John Jay wrote, "and to deny that
blessing to others involves an inconsistency not to be excused." Until America

ridded herself of human bondage, "her prayers to Heaven for liberty will be impious."

During the Revolution, official pronouncements reiterated the incompatibility of slavery and the struggle for independence. In Pennsylvania, for example, the Executive Council suggested to the Assembly in 1778 that the further importation of slaves be prohibited as a first step toward eventual abolition. Such a move, the Council pointed out, would not only be humane and just but would raise American prestige among the Europeans, "who are astonished to see a people eager for Liberty holding Negroes in Bondage." One year later, the Council contended that slavery disgraced a people supposedly fighting for liberty and urged a plan for gradual abolition. In 1780, the state legislature incorporated these sentiments in the preamble to a gradual-abolition act. Inasmuch as Americans had gone to war to obtain their freedom, the legislature asserted, such a blessing should be shared with those who had been and were being subjected to a similar state of bondage. In neighboring New Jersey, the governor urged the legislature in 1778 to provide for gradual abolition on the grounds that slavery conflicted with the principles of Christianity and was especially "odious and disgraceful" for a people professing to idolize liberty.

Perhaps the most radical extension of the Revolutionary ideology to Negro rights was made in New York. In 1785, the New York legislature passed a gradual-abolition act. The Council of Revision, however, rejected the bill because of a clause which prohibited Negroes from exercising the franchise. Contending that the freedmen should be granted full citizenship, the Council found this clause contrary to basic liberties and "repugnant to the principle on which the United States justify their separation from Great Britain," for it "supposes that those may rightfully be charged with the burdens of government, who have no representative share in imposing them." If free Negroes failed to secure the vote, the Council warned, a time might come when they would be numerous, wealthy,

and powerful, and they might then turn against a constitution which deprived them of their just rights. The legislature failed to override the Council's veto and delayed gradual abolition for another fourteen years.

Massachusetts, where resistance to British authority had been the most dramatic and far-reaching, perhaps reflected most clearly the troublesome conflict between the Revolutionary ideals and slavery. Few public pronouncements had been made on the subject of Negro bondage, Dr. Jeremy Belknap of Boston recalled, "till we began to feel the weight of oppression from 'our mother country' as Britain was then called. The inconsistency of pleading for our own rights and liberties, whilst we encouraged the subjugation of others, was very apparent; and from that time, both slavery and the slave-trade began to be discountenanced." Early in the Revolutionary struggle, James Otis struck at both colonial and Negro bondage. Although *The Rights of the British Colonies Asserted and Proved* has had more enduring fame as a forceful statement of the colonial constitutional position, that same tract applied John Locke's natural-rights philosophy not only to the current troubles with England but also to Negro slavery. "It is a clear truth," Otis wrote, "that those who every day barter away other mens liberty, will soon care little for their own."

As the colonial crisis became more intense and headed for a showdown, many New Englanders felt even more conscious of the inconsistency of opposing English tyranny and practicing slavery. "It always appeared a most iniquitous scheme to me," Abigail Adams wrote her husband in 1774, "to fight ourselves for what we are daily robbing and plundering from those who have as good a right to freedom as we have." Massachusetts town meetings began to couple their protests against royal and Parliamentary usurpation with pleas that slavery be abolished. Two months after the Declaration of Independence, the state house of representatives climaxed this growing sentiment by resolving that human bondage violated the natural rights of man and was "utterly inconsistent with the avowed principles in which this and other States have carried on their struggle for liberty." Meanwhile, several Massachusetts towns did not wait for legislative or judicial action but simply voted to have no slaves in their midst and to bear any expense that might arise from the emancipated Negroes' old age, infirmities, or inability to support themselves. By the end of 1776, one observer wrote, public opinion had virtually extirpated slavery.

In Massachusetts, unlike Pennsylvania, New Jersey, and New York, court action legally ended slavery. Prior to 1783, several slaves collected money among themselves and successfully sued for their freedom. Some even secured compensation for their services. John Adams, who represented several bondsmen in such cases, recalled that he "never knew a jury, by a verdict, to determine a negro to be a slave. They always found them free." Those arguments most commonly used to obtain a Negro's freedom, Adams stated, were based on "the rights of mankind, which was the fashionable word at that time." Successful court action encouraged the voluntary liberation of other slaves. To avoid court litigation, some slaves simply took the new constitution at its word when it affirmed the freedom and equality of all men, and either asked for and received their release or took it without consent.

Against this favorable background, the Massachusetts Supreme Court dealt Negro slavery a final blow. Quork Walker, a Negro slave, claimed his freedom on the basis of his master's verbal promise. Although this would ordinarily have been insufficient evidence to release him from bondage, Walker's attorneys found other grounds, the most important of which stressed the natural rights of man, the newly adopted Massachusetts Declaration of Rights, and the need for a more consistent stand against tyranny. "Can we expect to triumph over G. Britain," counsel Levi Lincoln asked, "to get free ourselves until we let those go free under us?" Chief Justice William Cushing's subsequent

charge to the jury reiterated much of this argument. Regardless of previous practices, he declared, the American people had demonstrated a greater devotion to the natural rights of man "and to that natural, innate desire of Liberty, with which Heaven (without regard to color, complexion, or shape of noses, features) has inspired all the human race." The new constitution, Cushing concluded, made this quite clear; consequently, "the idea of slavery is inconsistent with our own conduct and Constitution." This decision, handed down in 1783, ended slavery in the Puritan Commonwealth.

Exploiting the abolition sentiment aroused by the Revolution, Negro slaves and their white allies sought to dramatize the conflict between colonial principles and practices. Obviously aware of the symbolic value of the War of Independence for the cause of emancipation, Negro petitioners claimed a natural, a God-given, right to freedom and asserted "that Every Principle from which America has Acted in the Cours of their unhappy Dificultes with Great Briton Pleads Stronger than A thousand arguments in favours of your petioners." In the New London *Gazette*, "a Negro" made this point even more forcefully,

Is not all oppression vile?
When you attempt your freedom to defend,
Is reason yours, and partially your friend?
Be not deceiv'd—for reason pleads for all
Who by invasion and oppression fall.
I live a slave, and am inslav'd by those
Who yet pretend with reason to oppose
All schemes oppressive; and the gods invoke
To curse with thunders the invaders yoke.
O mighty God! let conscience seize the mind
Of Inconsistent men, who wish to find
A partial god to vindicate their cause,
And plead their freedom, while they break
    its laws.

If such theoretical or poetic appeals did not suffice, an estimated five thousand Negroes—most of them northerners—fought with white men for American independence. Despite colonial laws excluding Negroes from the militia and an early hesitancy to enlist them in the war, military expediency finally broke down these barriers and prompted the

Continental Congress and most of the states to enlist slaves and free Negroes. Between 1775 and 1781, Negro soldiers participated in virtually every major military action. In return for their military services, most states either freed them upon enlistment or at the end of hostilities.

In several states, religious organizations played an active and sometimes decisive role in the work of emancipation. After all, the pulpit was still a most influential and authoritative position from which to mold public opinion. Colonial parishioners had long been indoctrinated with the ideas of John Locke and their implications for the struggle with the mother country. Consistency and moral rectitude demanded, many churchmen insisted, that the laws of God and Nature also be directed at the glaring sin of human slavery. Otherwise the Revolutionary struggle had little significance. "Would we enjoy liberty?" a Massachusetts minister asked in 1774. "Then we must grant it to others. For shame, let us either cease to enslave our fellow men, or else let us cease to complain of those, that would enslave us." Quoting directly from the Scriptures, one churchman deplored the inconsistency of colonial practices and professions: "Happy is he saith the apostle Paul that condemneth not himself in that thing which he alloweth."

Most conspicuous among the antislavery religious groups were the Quakers. Abolition sentiment in Pennsylvania, for example, resulted largely from early and persistent Quaker opposition to slavery as inconsistent with the true spirit of Christianity. In 1758, the Philadelphia Yearly Meeting voted to exclude anyone who bought or sold slaves from participation in the meetings and affairs of the church; in 1774, it increased the penalty to disownment, and two years later it directed its members to "testify their disunion" with any member who resisted a last entreaty to free his slaves. The Quaker anti-slavery stand was not limited to any one state, however. Following the lead of Pennsylvania, yearly meetings in New England, New York, Baltimore, Virginia, and North Carolina soon adopted similar condemnations of slaveholding. After completing their work of emancipation, Quakers shifted their attention to improving the educational and economic level of the free Negro population.

Quakers also participated actively in the organization, leadership, and activities of the Pennsylvania Society for the Abolition of Slavery. Organized in 1775, the Society first directed its efforts toward securing an abolition law in Pennsylvania and protecting the free Negro from being kidnaped and sold into slavery. The victims of kidnaping were usually ignorant of legal remedies or unable to secure competent legal assistance. After a successful campaign for adequate protective legislation, the Society helped to enforce the new laws through the organization of committees of correspondence and by hiring competent counsel to secure the conviction of offenders. Although the Society suspended its work during the war, individual members continued to be active. Reorganized in 1787 as the Pennsylvania Society for Promoting the Abolition of Slavery, the Relief of Free Negroes Unlawfully Held in Bondage, and for Improving the Condition of the African Race, the Society joined the Quakers in granting assistance to freedmen.

In celebrating the abolition of slavery in New York, a Negro leader singled out for particular praise the Quakers and the New York Manumission Society, which he termed "the most powerful lever, or propelling cause." That society had organized in 1785 with John Jay as president and Alexander Hamilton as vice-president, thus reflecting the strong Federalist interest in abolition. As early as 1777, Jay had felt that Revolutionary consistency required the abolition of Negro bondage; twenty-two years later, as governor, Jay signed a bill providing for the gradual emancipation of New York's twenty-one thousand slaves. Having fulfilled its major goal, the Manumission Society concerned itself with enforcing and liberalizing the provisions of the abolition act and also joined with the

Pennsylvania Society to secure improved anti-kidnaping laws and educational facilities for free Negroes.

By 1830, whether by legislative, judicial, or constitutional action, Negro slavery had been virtually abolished in the North. Only 3,568 Negroes remained in bondage, and more than two-thirds of these resided in New Jersey. Although the Revolutionary ideology had also penetrated the South, particularly Virginia, emancipation had made little headway there. Powerful social and economic factors, the most obvious being Eli Whitney's cotton gin, made slavery the cheapest and most productive form of labor in the South. During the Revolution, some southerners had indeed joined with their northern compatriots to deplore the inconsistency of slavery and the struggle for liberty, but the postwar years brought only disappointment and finally complete disillusionment. After congratulating New England on its successful elimination of bondage, one Virginia judge sadly confessed in 1795 that deep-rooted white prejudices, the fear of large numbers of free Negroes, the impossibility of assimilating them into white society, and the need for a large and cheap servile labor force had combined to frustrate and defeat any plan for gradual abolition. "If, in Massachusetts," he wrote, "where the numbers are comparatively very small, this prejudice be discernable, how much stronger may it be imagined in this country, where every white man felt himself born to tyrannize, where the blacks were regarded as of no more importance than the brute cattle, where the laws rendered even venial offences criminal in them, where every species of degradation towards them was exercised on all occasions, and where even their lives were exposed to the ferocity of the masters." By the turn of the century, human bondage had become a "peculiar institution."

Freedom did not suddenly confer citizenship on the Negro. Emancipation, although enthusiastically welcomed by the northern slave, had its limitations. Until the post-Civil War era, in fact, most northern whites would maintain a careful distinction between granting Negroes legal protection—a theoretical right to life, liberty, and property—and political and social equality. No statute or court decision could immediately erase from the public mind, North or South, that long and firmly held conviction that the African race was inferior and therefore incapable of being assimilated politically, socially, and most certainly physically with the dominant and superior white society. Despite the absence of slavery in the North, one observer remarked, "chains of a stronger kind still manacled their limbs, from which no legislative act could free them; a mental and moral subordination and inferiority, to which tyrant custom has here subjected all the sons and daughters of Africa."

Kenneth M. Stampp

CHATTELS PERSONAL

In the nineteenth century the laws pertaining to slavery and race relations underwent a variety of changes, so that the distinction between slaves and free Negroes was undermined in the South. Ironically, it appears that as racism became more pronounced, the legal codes were providing increased recognition of the humanity of slaves. This selection from Stampp's classic study *The Peculiar Institution* illustrates the ambiguity and tension of race relations as they were reflected in law. Professor Stampp is Morrison Professor of History at the University of California, Berkeley.

IN Alabama's legal code of 1852 two clauses, standing in significant juxtaposition, recognized the dual character of the slave.[1]

The first clause confirmed his status as property—the right of the owner to his "time, labor and services" and to his obedient compliance with all lawful commands. Slavery thus being established by law, masters relied upon the state to use its power against white men who "tampered" with their bondsmen, and against bondsmen they could not subdue. Courts, police, and militia were indispensable parts of the machinery of control.

The second clause acknowledged the slave's status as a person. The law required that masters be humane to their slaves, furnish them adequate food and clothing, and provide care for them during sickness and in old age. In short, the state endowed masters with obligations as well as rights and assumed some responsibility for the welfare of the bondsmen.

But legislators and magistrates were caught in a dilemma whenever they found that the slave's status as property was incompatible with his status as a person. Individual masters struggled with this dilemma in different ways, some conceding much to the dictates of humanity, others demanding the utmost return from their investment. Olmsted explained the problem succinctly: "It is difficult to handle simply as property, a creature possessing human passions and human feelings, . . . while, on the other hand, the absolute necessity of dealing with property as a thing, greatly embarrasses a man in any attempt to treat it as a person."[2]

After adopting Draconian codes in the early eighteenth century, the various legislatures in some respects gradually humanized them, while the courts tempered their application, but there was no way to resolve the contradiction implicit in the very term "human property." Both legislators and judges frequently appeared erratic in dealing with bondsmen as both *things* and *persons*. Alabama's code defined the property status of the slave before acknowledging his human status, and throughout the ante-bellum South the cold language of statutes and judicial decisions made it evident that, legally, the slave was less a person than a thing.

[1] Extracts from the slave codes presented in this chapter were taken from the legal codes or revised statutes of the southern states. See also Hurd, *Law of Freedom and Bondage*, and the various studies of slavery in individual states.

[2] Olmsted, *Back Country*, p. 64.

The fact that southern slavery was, in the main, Negro slavery gave an advantage to those who wished to preserve it. If he ran away, the Negro slave with his distinctive skin color could not so easily escape detection as could a white indentured servant. Moreover, all Negroes were brought to America in bondage, and legislatures soon adopted the principle of *partus sequitur ventrem*—the child inherits the condition of the mother. Therefore, the English common-law presumption in favor of freedom did not apply to Negroes; in all the slave states (except Delaware) the presumption was that people with black skins were slaves unless they could prove that they were free. Any strange Negro found in a southern community without "freedom papers" was arrested as a fugitive.

But southern slavery was not *exclusively* Negro slavery. The status of a child of mixed Negro and white ancestry depended upon the status of the mother. The offspring of a Negro slave father and a free white mother was free. The offspring of a free white father and a Negro, mulatto, quadroon, or octoroon slave mother was a slave. In fact, the Texas Supreme Court once ruled that the child of a slave mother was a slave no matter how remote the Negro ancestry.[3] Hence some slaves were whites by any rational definition as well as by all outward appearances, even though some distant female ancestor may have been a Negro. One Virginia fugitive had a "complexion so nearly white, that . . . a stranger would suppose there was no African blood in him."[4]

Not all southern slaves were Negroes, and not all southern masters were whites. In 1830, more than thirty-six hundred free Negroes or persons of mixed ancestry owned slaves. The great majority of these colored slaveowners had merely purchased husbands, wives, or children and were unable to emancipate them under existing state laws. A few were substantial planters, such as the Negro in King George County, Virginia, who owned seventy-one slaves; another in St. Landry Parish, Louisiana,

who owned seventy-five; and two others in Colleton District, South Carolina, who owned eighty-four apiece. Though southern whites overwhelmingly disapproved, only in Delaware and Arkansas did the courts refuse to sanction the ownership of slaves by "free persons of color." The Arkansas Supreme Court held that slavery had its foundation "in an *inferiority of race*," and the bondage of one Negro to another lacked "this solid foundation to rest upon."[5]

Since Negroes were presumed to be slaves and whites were presumed to be free, the southern states found it essential in cases of mixed ancestry to decide who were to be treated as Negroes and who as whites. No state adopted the principle that "a single drop of Negro blood" made a person legally a member of the "inferior race." Each state prescribed the proportion of Negro ancestry which excluded a person from the privileges enjoyed by white men. . . .

Any person with Negro ancestors too remote to cause him to be classified as a mulatto was by law a white man. While such a person could be held as a slave, the burden of proof was placed upon the putative master. In Kentucky, affirmed the Court of Appeals, "it has been well settled, that . . . having less than a fourth of African blood, is *prima facie* evidence of freedom." A Virginia jury having found that a woman suing for her freedom was white, it was incumbent upon her master to prove that she "was descended in the maternal line from a slave. Having not proved it, she and her children must be considered free."[7]

Some slaveholders preferred to use "bright mulattoes" as domestics; a few paid premium prices for light-skinned females to be used as concubines or prostitutes. But most masters saw the inconvenience of owning slaves who were nearly white: the presumption of freedom in their favor, and the greater ease with which they could escape. One former bondsman, a "white man with blue eyes," recalled his master's repeated at-

---

[3] Catterall (ed.), *Judicial Cases*, V, p. 295.
[4] Richmond *Enquirer*, February 7, 1837.

[5] Carter G. Woodson, *Free Negro Owners of Slaves in the United States in 1830* (Washington, D.C., 1924); Catterall (ed.), *Judicial Cases*, IV, p. 215; V, p. 257.
[7] Catterall (ed.), *Judicial Cases*, I, pp. 121, 330.

tempts to sell him, always unsuccessful. A Kentucky slave, "owing to his being almost white, and to the consequent facilities of escape," was adjudged to be worth only "half as much as other slaves of the ordinary color and capacities."[8] Here was convincing evidence of the importance of racial visibility in keeping the Negro in bondage.

* * *

Every slave state had a slave code. Besides establishing the property rights of those who owned human chattels, these codes supported masters in maintaining discipline and provided safeguards for the white community against slave rebellions. In addition, they held slaves, as thinking beings, morally responsible and punishable for misdemeanors and felonies.

Fundamentally the slave codes were much alike. Those of the Deep South were somewhat more severe than those of the Upper South, but most of the variations were in minor details. The similarities were due, in part, to the fact that new states patterned their codes after those of the old. South Carolina's code of 1712 was almost a copy of the Barbadian code; Georgia's code of 1770 duplicated South Carolina's code of 1740; and later the Gulf states borrowed heavily from both. In the Upper South, Tennessee virtually adopted North Carolina's code, while Kentucky and Missouri lifted many passages from Virginia's. But the similarities were also due to the fact that slavery, wherever it existed, made necessary certain kinds of regulatory laws. The South Carolina code would probably have been essentially the same if the Barbadian code had never been written.

After a generation of liberalization following the American Revolution, the codes underwent a reverse trend toward increasing restrictions. This trend was clearly evident by the 1820's, when rising slave prices and expansion into the Southwest caused more and more Southerners to accept slavery as a permanent

institution. The Nat Turner rebellion and northern abolitionist attacks merely accelerated a trend which had already begun. . . .

At the heart of every code was the requirement that slaves submit to their masters and respect all white men. The Louisiana code of 1806 proclaimed this most lucidly: "The condition of the slave being merely a passive one, his subordination to his master and to all who represent him is not susceptible of modification or restriction . . . he owes to his master, and to all his family, a respect without bounds, and an absolute obedience, and he is consequently to execute all the orders which he receives from him, his said master, or from them." A slave was neither to raise his hand against a white man nor to use insulting or abusive language. Any number of acts, said a North Carolina judge, may constitute "insolence"—it may be merely "a look, the pointing of a finger, a refusal or neglect to step out of the way when a white person is seen to approach. But each of such acts violates the rules of propriety, and if tolerated, would destroy that subordination, upon which our social system rests."[6]

The codes rigidly controlled the slave's movements and his communication with others. A slave was not to be "at large" without a pass which he must show to any white man who asked to see it; if he forged a pass or free papers he was guilty of a felony. Except in a few localities, he was prohibited from hiring his own time, finding his own employment, or living by himself. A slave was not to preach, except to his master's own slaves on his master's premises in the presence of whites. A gathering of more than a few slaves (usually five) away from home, unattended by a white, was an "unlawful assembly" regardless of its purpose or orderly decorum.

No person, not even the master, was to teach a slave to read or write, employ him in setting type in a printing office, or give him books or pamphlets. A religious publication asked rhetorically: "Is there any great moral reason why we should

---

[8] Drew, *The Refugee*, pp. 123–32; Catterall (ed.), *Judicial Cases*, I, p. 278.

[6] Catterall (ed.), *Judicial Cases*, II, p. 168.

incur the tremendous risk of having our wives slaughtered in consequence of our slaves being taught to read incendiary publications?" They did not need to read the Bible to find salvation: "Millions of those now in heaven never owned a bible."[7]

Farms and plantations employing slaves were to be under the supervision of resident white men, and not left to the sole direction of slave foremen. Slaves were not to beat drums, blow horns, or possess guns; periodically their cabins were to be searched for weapons. They were not to administer drugs to whites or practice medicine. "A slave under pretence of practicing medicine," warned a Tennessee judge, "might convey intelligence from one plantation to another, of a contemplated insurrectionary movement; and thus enable the slaves to act in concert."[8]

A slave was not to possess liquor, or purchase it without a written order from his owner. He was not to trade without a permit, or gamble with whites or with other slaves. He was not to raise cotton, swine, horses, mules, or cattle. Allowing a slave to own animals, explained the North Carolina Supreme Court, tended "to make other slaves dissatisfied . . . and thereby excite . . . a spirit of insubordination."[9]

Southern cities and towns supplemented the state codes with additional regulations. Most of them prohibited slaves from being on the streets after curfew or living in dwellings separate from their masters. Richmond required Negroes and mulattoes to step aside when whites passed by, and barred them from riding in carriages except in the capacity of menials. Charleston slaves could not swear, smoke, walk with a cane, assemble at military parades, or make joyful demonstrations. In Washington, North Carolina, the town Commissioners prohibited "all disorderly shouting and dancing, and all disorderly . . . assemblies . . . of slaves and free Negroes in the streets, market and other public places." In Natchez, all "strange slaves" had to leave the city by four o'clock on Sunday afternoon.[1]

Violations of the state and local codes were misdemeanors or felonies subject to punishment by justices, sheriffs, police, and constabulary. Whipping was the most common form of public punishment for less than capital offenses. Except in Louisiana, imprisonment was rare. By mid-nineteenth century branding and mutilation had declined, though they had not been abolished everywhere. South Carolina did not prohibit branding until 1833, and occasionally thereafter slave felons still had their ears cropped. Mississippi and Alabama continued to enforce the penalty of "burning in the hand" for felonies not capitally punished.[2]

But most slave offenders were simply tied up in the jail or at a whipping post and flogged. Some states in the Upper South limited to thirty-nine the number of stripes that could be administered at any one time, though more could be given in a series of whippings over a period of days or weeks. In the Deep South floggings could legally be more severe. Alabama permitted up to one hundred stripes on the bare back of a slave who forged a pass or engaged in "riots, routs, unlawful assemblies, trespasses, and seditious speeches."

State criminal codes dealt more severely with slaves and free Negroes than with whites. In the first place, they made certain acts felonies when committed by Negroes but not when committed by whites; and in the second place, they assigned heavier penalties to Negroes than whites convicted of the same offense. Every southern state defined a substantial number of felonies carrying capital punishment for slaves and lesser punishments for whites. In addition to murder of any degree, slaves received the death penalty for attempted murder, manslaughter, rape and attempted rape

---

[7] *Southern Presbyterian*, quoted in *De Bow's Review*, XVIII (1855), p. 52; *Farmers' Register*, IV (1836), p. 181.
[8] Catterall (ed.), *Judicial Cases*, II, pp. 520–21.
[9] *Ibid.*, II, pp. 240–41.

[1] *Ibid.*, II, p. 182; Henry, *Police Control*, p. 48; [Ingraham], *South-West*, II, pp. 72–73; Phillips, *American Negro Slavery*, pp. 497–98.
[2] Henry, *Police Control*, p. 52; Sydnor, *Slavery in Mississippi*, p. 83.

upon a white woman, rebellion and attempted rebellion, poisoning, robbery, and arson. A battery upon a white person might also carry a sentence of death under certain circumstances. In Louisiana, a slave who struck his master, a member of the master's family, or the overseer, "so as to cause a contusion, or effusion or shedding of blood," was to suffer death—as was a slave on a third conviction for striking a white.

The codes were quite unmerciful toward whites who interfered with slave discipline. Heavy fines were levied upon persons who unlawfully traded with slaves, sold them liquor without the master's permission, gave them passes, gambled with them, or taught them to read or write. North Carolina made death the penalty for concealing a slave "with the intent and for the purpose of enabling such slave to escape." Aiding or encouraging a bondsman to rebel was the most heinous crime of all. "If a free person," said the Alabama code, "advise or conspire with a slave to . . . make insurrection, . . . he shall be punished with death, whether such rebellion or insurrection be made or not."

Every slave state made it a felony to say or write anything that might lead, directly or indirectly, to discontent or rebellion. In 1837, the Missouri legislature passed an act "to prohibit the publication, circulation, and promulgation of the abolition doctrines." The Virginia code of 1849 provided a fine and imprisonment for any person who maintained "that owners have not right of property in their slaves." Louisiana made it a capital offense to use "language in any public discourse, from the bar, the bench, the stage, the pulpit, or in any place whatsoever" that might produce "insubordination among the slaves." Most southern states used their police power to prohibit the circulation of "incendiary" material through the United States mail; on numerous occasions local postmasters, public officials, or mobs seized and destroyed antislavery publications.

Southerners justified these seizures on the ground that some slaves were literate in spite of the laws against teaching them to read. A petition to the South Carolina legislature claimed that "the ability to read exists on probably every plantation in the State; and it is utterly impossible for even the *masters* to prevent this—as is apparent from the cases in which servants learn to write by stealth." But whether or not slaves could read, the "corrupting influence" of antislavery propaganda was bound to reach them unless it was suppressed. There seemed to be no choice but to construct an "intellectual blockade" against ideas hostile to slavery if property were to be protected and the peace of society secured. Hence the laws controlled the voices and pens of white men as well as black.[3] . . .

Southern slave codes protected the owners of bondsmen who attempted to abscond by requiring officers to assist in their recapture and by giving all white men power to arrest them. . . .

Occasionally a band of runaways was too formidable to be dispersed by volunteers, and the governor called upon the militia to capture or destroy it. Ordinarily, however, this and other organized police activity was delegated to the slave patrols. A system of patrols, often more or less loosely connected with the militia, existed in every slave state. Virginia empowered each county or corporation court to "appoint, for a term not exceeding three months, one or more patrols" to visit "all negro quarters and other places suspected of having therein unlawful assemblies," and to arrest "such slaves as may stroll from one plantation to another without permission." Alabama compelled every slaveowner under sixty and every nonslaveholder under forty-five to perform patrol duty. The justices of each precinct divided the eligible males into detachments which had to patrol at least one night a week during their terms of service. Everywhere the patrols played a major role in the system of control. . . .

The final clauses in the southern legal codes relating directly to the control of

---

[3] Undated petition from Chester District, South Carolina Slavery Manuscripts Collection; Clement Eaton, *Freedom of Thought in the Old South* (Durham, 1940), *passim*.

slaves were those governing free Negroes. The laws reflected the general opinion that these people were an anomaly, a living denial "that nature's God intended the African for the *status* of slavery." They "embitter by their presence the happiness of those who remain slaves. They entice them and furnish them with facilities to elope." They were potential allies of the slaves in the event of a rebellion. In 1830, David Walker, a free Negro who moved from North Carolina to Boston, wrote and attempted to circulate in the South a pamphlet which urged the slaves to fight for their freedom. He thus aroused southern legislatures to the menace of the free Negro.[9]

The trend of ante-bellum legislation was toward ever more stringent controls. Free Negroes could not move from one state to another, and those who left their own state for any purpose could not return. In South Carolina and the Gulf states Negro seamen were arrested and kept in custody while their vessels were in port. Though free Negroes could make contracts and own property, in most other respects their civil rights were as circumscribed as those of slaves. They were the victims of the white man's fears, of racial prejudice, and of the desire to convince slaves that winning freedom was scarcely worth the effort.

Many Southerners desired the complete expulsion of the free Negroes, or the re-enslavement of those who would not leave. Petitions poured in to the state legislatures demanding laws that would implement one or the other of these policies. In 1849, a petition from Augusta County, Virginia, asked the legislature to make an appropriation for a program of gradual removal; all free Negroes who refused to go to Liberia should be expelled from the state within five years.[1] In 1859, the Arkansas legislature required sheriffs to order the state's handful of free Negroes to leave. Those who remained were to be hired out as slaves for a year, after which those who still remained were to be sold into permanent bondage.

A Texas editor caught the spirit of the extreme proslavery element during the 1850's when he proclaimed that the time was "near at hand for determined action." Southern free Negroes were "destined to be remitted back into slavery," which was their "true condition."[2] In this last ante-bellum decade most states adopted laws authorizing the "voluntary enslavement" of these people and enabling them to select their own masters. Virginia went a step further and permitted the sale into "absolute slavery" of free Negroes convicted of offenses "punishable by confinement in the penitentiary"; Florida applied the same penalty to those who were "idle" or "dissolute." This problem, some apparently felt, would remain unsolved until all Negroes and "mulattoes" were not only *presumed* to be slaves but were in *fact* slaves.

"A slave," said a Tennessee judge, "is not in the condition of a horse. . . . He has mental capacities, and an immortal principle in his nature." The laws did not "extinguish his high-born nature nor deprive him of many rights which are inherent in man."[3] All the southern codes recognized the slave as a person for purposes other than holding him accountable for crimes. Many state constitutions required the legislature "to pass such laws as may be necessary to oblige the owners of slaves to treat them with humanity; to provide for them necessary clothing and provisions; [and] to abstain from all injuries to them, extending to life or limb."

The legislatures responded with laws extending some protection to the persons of slaves. Masters who refused to feed and clothe slaves properly might be fined; in several states the court might order them to be sold, the proceeds going to the dispossessed owners. Those who abandoned or neglected insane, aged, or infirm slaves were also liable to fines. In Virginia the overseers of the poor

[9] Jackson *Mississippian*, February 26, 1858; Tallahassee *Floridian and Journal*, April 11, 1857; *American Farmer*, XI (1829), p. 167; Johnson, *Ante-Bellum North Carolina*, pp. 515–16.
[1] Virginia Legislative Petitions.

[2] Austin *Texas State Gazette*, September 12, 1857.
[3] Catterall (ed.), *Judicial Cases*, II, p. 530.

were required to care for such slaves and to charge their masters.

Now and then a master was tried and convicted for the violation of one of these laws. . . . But prosecutions were infrequent. Since a slave could neither file a complaint nor give evidence against his master, action depended upon the willingness of whites to testify in the slave's behalf. This happened only under unusual circumstances.

Some of the codes regulated the hours of labor. As early as 1740, South Carolina limited the working day to fifteen hours from March to September and fourteen hours from September to March. All the codes forbade field labor on Sunday. In Virginia, a master who worked his slaves on Sunday, "except in household or other work of necessity or charity," was to be fined two dollars for each offense. It was permissible, however, to let slaves labor on the Sabbath for wages; and the North Carolina Supreme Court ruled that it was not an indictable offense to give them Sunday tasks as a punishment.[5] With rare exceptions, masters who were so inclined violated these laws with impunity.

The early colonial codes had assessed only light penalties, or none at all, for killing a slave. South Carolina, "to restrain and prevent barbarity being exercised toward slaves," provided, in 1740, that a white who willfully murdered a slave was to be punished by a fine of seven hundred pounds or imprisonment at hard labor for seven years. Killing a slave in "sudden heat or passion" or by "undue correction" carried a fine of three hundred and fifty pounds. In Georgia prior to 1770, and in North Carolina prior to 1775, taking a slave's life was not a felony.

After the American Revolution there was a drastic change of policy. Virginia, in 1788, and North Carolina, in 1791, defined the malicious killing of a slave as murder subject to the same penalty imposed upon the murderer of a freeman. In 1817, North Carolina applied this principle to persons convicted of manslaughter. Georgia's Constitution of 1798

[5] *Ibid.*, II, p. 107.

contained a clause that was copied, in substance, into the constitutions of several states in the Southwest: "Any person who shall maliciously dismember or deprive a slave of life shall suffer such punishment as would be inflicted in case the like offence had been committed on a free white person."

Eventually all the southern states adopted laws of this kind. . . .

By the 1850's, most of the codes had made cruelty a public offense even when not resulting in death. . . .

But these laws invariably had significant qualifications. For example, the accidental death of a slave while receiving "moderate correction" was not homicide. Killing a slave in the act of rebellion or when resisting legal arrest was always "justifiable homicide." South Carolina permitted a white person to "apprehend and moderately correct" a slave who was at large without a pass and refused to submit to examination; "and if any such slave shall assault and strike such white person, such slave may be lawfully killed." The South Carolina law against cruelty concluded with a nullifying clause: "nothing herein contained shall be so construed as to prevent the owner or person having charge of any slave from inflicting on such slave such punishment as may be necessary for the good government of the same." Southern courts, by their interpretations of the laws, in effect added further qualifications. Thus the North Carolina Supreme Court ruled that a homicide upon a slave did not require as much provocation as a homicide upon a white to make it jusifiable.

Under most circumstances a slave was powerless to defend himself from an assault by a white man. According to the Tennessee Supreme Court, severe chastisement by the master did not justify resistance. If a master exercised his right to punish, "with or without cause, [and] the slave resist and slay him, it is murder . . . because the law cannot recognize the violence of the master as a legitimate cause of provocation." According to the Georgia Supreme Court, even if the owner should "exceed the bounds of reason . . . in his chastisement, the

slave must submit . . . unless the attack
. . . be calculated to produce death."[6] . . .

In a few notable cases the courts enforced the laws against the killing of
slaves. A North Carolinian was sentenced to death for the murder of his
own female chattel. Over a period of
months he had "beat her with clubs, iron
chains, and other deadly weapons, time
after time; burnt her; inflicted stripes . . .
which literally excoriated her whole
body." The court held him "justly an-
swerable" for her death, though he did
not "specially design it." . . .

Decisions such as these were exceptional. Only a handful of whites suffered
capital punishment for murdering
slaves, and they were usually persons
who had committed the offense upon
slaves not their own. When a master was
convicted, it was generally for a lesser
crime, such as killing in "sudden heat or
passion" or by "undue correction." And a
convicted killer, whether or not the master, rarely received as heavy a penalty as
he would have for a homicide upon a
white.

Actually, the great majority of whites
who, by a reasonable interpretation of
the law, were guilty of feloniously killing slaves escaped without any punishment at all. Of those who were indicted,
most were either acquitted or never
brought to trial. For several reasons this
was almost inevitable.

One major reason was that neither
slaves nor free Negroes could testify
against whites. There were, as one
Southerner observed, "a thousand inci-
dents of plantation life concealed from
public view," witnessed only by slaves,
which the law could not reach. One of
slavery's "most vulnerable points," a de-
fender of the institution agreed, was the
"helpless position of the slave" when his
master was "placed in opposition to
him." His "mouth being closed as a witness," he had to depend upon whites to
testify in his behalf.[9]

But here was the second major ob-

stacle in the way of convictions: white
witnesses were reluctant to testify
against white offenders. Most white men
were obsessed with the terrible urgency
of racial solidarity, with the fear that the
whole complex mechanism of control
would break down if the master's discre-
tion in governing slaves were questioned. It took a particularly shocking
atrocity to break through this barrier
—to enable a white man to win the approval of his neighbors for giving evidence against another white. A North
Carolinian knew of "a number" of instances in which "nobody in the neigh-
borhood had any doubt that the death of
the slave was caused by the severity of
his treatment," but no guilty party was
indicted or brought to trial. Frederick
Douglass cited the case of a Maryland
woman who murdered a slave with a
piece of firewood. A warrant was issued
for her arrest, but it was never served.[1]

There was still a third obstacle. Even
when whites agreed to testify, there remained the problem of getting a white
jury to convict. . . . The foreman of a
South Carolina jury declared frankly
that he "would not convict the defend-
ant, or any other white person, of murdering a slave."[2] This was the feeling of
most jurymen. . . .

The fate of a slave who was the principal, rather than the victim, of an alleged misdemeanor or felony was highly
uncertain. The state codes established
regular judicial procedures for the trial
of slaves accused of public offenses, but
probably most minor offenses, such as
petit larceny, were disposed of without
resort to the courts. For instance, when
an Alabama slave was caught stealing
from a neighboring plantation, the pro-
prietor agreed not to prosecute if the
overseer punished the slave himself. The
state Supreme Court sanctioned the informal settlement of such cases. Even
though an offense was "criminally punishable," said the court, so far as the
public was concerned it was better to

[6] Catterall (ed.), *Judicial Cases*, II, pp. 549–50;
III, pp. 35–36.
[9] Henry, *Police Control*, p. 79; Thomas R. R.
Cobb, *An Inquiry into the Law of Negro Slavery
in the United States of America* (Philadelphia,
1858), pp. 97–98.

[1] Bassett, *Slavery in North Carolina*, pp. 91–92;
Douglass, *My Bondage*, pp. 125–26.
[2] Davis (ed.), *Diary of Bennet H. Barrow*, p. 148;
Gavin Diary, entries for November 4, 16, 1857;
Catterall (ed.), *Judicial Cases*, II, p. 343.

have the punishment "admeasured by a domestic tribunal."[5]

Nevertheless, many bondsmen who violated the law were given public trials. In colonial days they were always arraigned before special "Negro courts," which were usually less concerned about the formalities of traditional English justice than about speedy verdicts and certain punishments. A slave accused of a capital offense, according to the South Carolina code of 1740, was to be tried "in the most summary and expeditious maner"; on conviction he was to suffer death by such means as would be "most effectual to deter others from offending in the like maner." Justice in the "Negro courts" was at best capricious.

For misdemeanors, and in some states for crimes not punished capitally, the summary processes of "Negro courts" survived until the abolition of slavery. . . .

In the nineteenth century, most states gave slaves jury trials in the regular courts when accused of capital crimes; some went further and gave them this privilege when accused of any felony. The Missouri Constitution of 1820 and the Texas Constitution of 1845 provided that in criminal cases slaves were to have an impartial trial by jury. On conviction, a Missouri slave was to suffer "the same degree of punishment, and no other, that would be inflicted on a free white person for a like offense." North Carolina slaves accused of capital offenses were tried in the superior courts, and the law required the trials to be conducted as the trials of freemen. In Alabama, they were tried before the circuit court of the county, "in the mode provided by law for the trial of white persons," except that two-thirds of the jurors had to be slaveholders. In Georgia, capital crimes continued to be tried before three justices until 1850, when the superior courts were given jurisdiction.

A few states never granted jury trial or abandoned the informal courts and summary procedures even in capital cases. . . .

Many Southerners trained in the law recognized the possibilities for miscar-

riages of justice in the "Negro courts." A South Carolina judge called these courts "the worst system that could be devised." In his message to the legislature, in 1833, Governor Robert Y. Hayne acknowledged that reform was "imperiously called for." "Capital offenses committed by slaves, involving the nicest questions of the law, are often tried by courts composed of persons ignorant of the law." . . . However, criticism such as this produced few reforms.

In practice, the quality of justice slaves received from juries and regular courts was not consistently better than the justice they received from "Negro courts." When tension was great and the passions of white men were running high, a slave found it as difficult to get a fair trial before a jury in one of the superior courts of North Carolina or Alabama as he did before the justices in one of the informal courts of South Carolina or Virginia. Nowhere, regardless of constitutional or statutory requirements, was the trial of a bondsman apt to be like the trial of a freeman. Though counsel was guaranteed, though jurors might be challenged, though Negroes could testify in cases involving members of their own race, the trial of a slave was never the trial of a man by his peers. Rather, it was the trial of a man with inferior rights by his superiors—of a man who was property as well as a person. Inevitably, most justices, judges, and jurors permitted questions of discipline and control to obscure considerations of even justice.

A slave accused of committing violence upon another slave, rather than upon a white, had a better chance for a fair trial. Here the deeper issues of discipline and racial subordination were not involved, and the court could hear the case calmly and decide it on its merits. Moreover, the penalty on conviction was usually relatively light. Slaves were capitally punished for the murder of other slaves almost as rarely as whites were capitally punished for the murder of slaves. . . .

The southern codes did not prescribe lighter penalties for slaves who murdered other slaves than for slaves who murdered whites. The theory of the law was that one offense was as serious as

[5] Catterall (ed.), *Judicial Cases*, III, pp. 158–59.

the other. But the white men who applied the law usually thought otherwise.

* * *

"A free African population is a curse to any country," the Chancellor of the South Carolina Court of Appeals once flatly affirmed. "This race, . . . in a state of freedom, and in the midst of a civilized community, are a dead weight to the progress of improvement." Free Negroes became "pilferers and maurauders," "consumers, without being producers . . . governed mainly by the instincts of animal nature."[6] Racial attitudes such as these, the fear of free Negroes as a social menace, and respect for the rights of property caused the southern states to adopt constitutional prohibitions against the legislative emancipation of slaves without the consent of their owners.

But the state constitutions put few obstacles in the way of masters who wished to manumit their own slaves. In the border states of Delaware, Maryland (until 1860), Kentucky, and Missouri, the sole legislative restrictions were that creditors' claims must be respected and that a manumitted slave must not become a burden to the public because of age or infirmity. Virginia added the further condition that a manumitted slave was not to remain in the state for more than a year "without lawful permission." A county or corporation court might grant this permission if it had evidence that the freedman was "of good character, sober, peaceable, orderly and industrious." In North Carolina an emancipated slave had to leave the state within ninety days, unless a superior court made an exception because of "meritorious service." In Tennessee a slave freed after 1831 had to be sent beyond her borders immediately; after 1854 he had to be sent to the west coast of Africa.

In the Deep South the trend was toward increasingly severe legislative restrictions. In Louisiana (for many years the most liberal of these states) an act of 1807 limited the privilege of manu-

mission to slaves who were at least thirty years old and who had not been guilty of bad conduct during the previous four years. In 1830, Louisiana required emancipated slaves to leave the state within thirty days; after 1852, they had to leave the United States within twelve months. Five years later, Louisiana entirely prohibited private emancipations within the state.

The remaining states of the lower South had outlawed private emancipations early in the nineteenth century, except when granted by a special act of the legislature as a reward for "meritorious service." . . . The South Carolina legislature purchased the freedom of two slaves and granted them annual pensions of fifty dollars for betraying insurrection plots. The Louisiana legislature emancipated a slave and gave him a reward of five hundred dollars for the same "meritorious service."[7] . . .

Several states in the Deep South . . . prohibited emancipation by last will and testament. South Carolina acted as early as 1841, when it voided all deeds and wills designed to free slaves before or after removal from the state. Mississippi, Georgia, Arkansas, and Alabama adopted similar laws during the next two decades.

Occasionally a testator attempted to circumvent the statutes against emancipation, but almost invariably the court invalidated his will. . . .

The truth was, of course, that *living* masters in all the southern states—even in those which prohibited manumission by last will and testament—always had the right to remove their slaves to a free state and there release them from bondage. Though no slave state could deprive them of this right, few made use of it.

Moreover, only a handful of slaveholders wrote wills providing for manumissions in states where this continued to be legal. An even smaller number would have done so in the Deep South

[6] Catterall (ed.), *Judicial Cases*, II, p. 442.

[7] Catterall (ed.), *Judicial Cases*, III, p. 21; Henry, *Police Control*, pp. 17–18; Taylor, "Negro Slavery in Louisiana," pp. 203–204. In 1860, Maryland also prohibited private emancipations within the state.

had the privilege remained open to them. In no slave state, early or late in the antebellum period, were the total yearly emancipations more than a small fraction of the natural increase of the slave population. For example, in 1859, only three thousand slaves were emancipated throughout the entire South. At that time both Virginia and Kentucky permitted manumissions by deed or will. Yet Virginia, with a slave population of a half million, freed only two hundred and seventy-seven; Kentucky, with a slave population of nearly a quarter million, freed only one hundred and seventy-six.

Clearly, if the decline of slavery were to await the voluntary acts of individuals, the time of its demise was still in the distant future. The failure of voluntary emancipation was evident long before the 1830's when, according to Judge Lumpkin, "the blind zealots of the North" began their "unwarrantable interference."[1] James H. Hammond got at the crux of the matter when he asked whether any people in history had ever voluntarily surrendered two billion dollars worth of property....

[1] Catterall (ed.), *Judicial Cases*, III, pp. 1–2.

III. SLAVERY AND SOCIETY

Frank Tannenbaum

SLAVE AND CITIZEN

Professor Tannenbaum, who taught for many years at Columbia, was the first scholar to attempt a broad comparison of slavery in North and South America. His book *Slave and Citizen: A History of the Negro in the Americas* has attracted a wide audience from the time it initially appeared in 1946. His general thesis—that differences in racial patterns stemmed from cultural rather than economic or demographic circumstances—has remained extremely persuasive to many historians, among them Stanley Elkins and Herbert S. Klein.

THIS adventure of the Negro in the New World has been structured differently in the United States than in the other parts of this hemisphere. In spite of his adaptability, his willingness, and his competence, in spite of his complete identification with the mores of the United States, he is excluded and denied. A barrier has been drawn against the Negro. This barrier has never been completely effective, but it has served to deny to him the very things that are of greatest value among us—equality of opportunity for growth and development as a man among men. The shadow of slavery is still cast ahead of us, and we behave toward the Negro as if the imputation of slavery had something of a slave by nature in it. The Emancipation may have legally freed the Negro, but it failed morally to free the white man, and by that failure it denied to the Negro the moral status requisite for effective legal freedom.

But this did not occur in the other parts of this world we call new and free. It did not occur because the very nature of the institution of slavery was developed in a different moral and legal setting, and in turn shaped the political and ethical biases that have manifestly separated the United States from the other parts of the New World in this re-spect. The separation is a moral one. We have denied ourselves the acceptance of the Negro as a man because we have denied him the moral competence to become one, and in that have challenged the religious, political, and scientific bases upon which our civilization and our scheme of values rest. This separation has a historical basis, and in turn it has molded the varied historical outcome.

The Negro slave arriving in the Iberian Peninsula in the middle of the fifteenth century found a propitious environment.[84] The setting, legal as well as

[84] Elizabeth Donnan, op. cit., Vol. I ("1441–1700," 1930), p. 29: "For as our people did not find them hardened in the belief of the other Moors, and saw how they came in unto the law of Christ with a good will, they made no difference between them and their free servants, born in our own country. But those whom they saw fitted for managing property, they set free and married to women who were natives of the land, making with them a division of their property, as if they had been bestowed on those who married them by the will of their own fathers, and for the merits of their service they were bound to act in a like manner. Yea, and some widows of good family who bought some of these female slaves, either adopted them or left them a portion of their estate by will, so that in the future they married right well, treating them as entirely free. Suffice it that I never saw one of these slaves put in irons like other captives, and scarcely any one who did not turn Christian and was not very gently treated." Quoted from *The Chronicle of the Discovery and Conquest of Guinea*, by Gomes Eannes de Azurara.

moral, that made this easy transition possible was due to the fact that the people of the Iberian Peninsula were not strangers to slavery. The institution of slavery, which had long since died out in the rest of western Europe, had here survived for a number of reasons, especially because of the continuing wars with the Moors, which lasted until the very year of the discovery of America.

*   *   *

But the mere survival of slavery in itself is perhaps less important than the persistence of a long tradition of slave law that had come down through the Justianian Code. The great codification of Spanish traditional law, which in itself summarizes the Mediterranean legal *mores* of many centuries, was elaborated by Alfonso the Wise between the years 1263 and 1265. In this code there is inherent belief in the equality of men under the law of nature, and slavery therefore is something against both nature and reason.

*   *   *

The slave had a body of law, protective of him as a human being, which was already there when the Negro arrived and had been elaborated long before he came upon the scene. And when he did come, the Spaniard may not have known him as a Negro, but the Spanish law and *mores* knew him as a slave and made him the beneficiary of the ancient legal heritage. This law provided, among other matters, for the following:

The slave might marry a free person if the slave status was known to the other party. Slaves could marry against the will of their master if they continued serving him as before. Once married, they could not be sold apart, except under conditions permitting them to live as man and wife. If the slave married a free person with the knowledge of his master, and the master did not announce the fact of the existing slave status, then the slave by that mere fact became free.[102] If married slaves owned

by separate masters could not live together because of distance, the church should persuade one or the other to sell his slave. If neither of the masters could be persuaded, the church was to buy one of them so that the married slaves could live together.[103] The children followed the status of their mother, and the child of a free mother remained free even if she later became a slave.[104] In spite of his full powers over his slave, the master might neither kill nor injure him unless authorized by the judge, nor abuse him against reason or nature, nor starve him to death. But if the master did any of these things, the slave could complain to the judge, and if the complaint were verified, the judge must sell him, giving the price to the owner, and the slave might never be returned to the original master.[105] Any Jewish or Moorish slave became free upon turning Christian, and even if the master himself later became a Christian, he recovered no rights over his former slave.[106]

*   *   *

Spanish law, custom, and tradition were transferred to America and came to govern the position of the Negro slave. It is interesting to note that a large body of new law was developed for the treatment of the Indians in America, whereas the Negro's position was covered by isolated *cedulas* dealing with special problems. It was not until 1789 that a formal code dealing with the Negro slave was promulgated.[120] But this new code, as recognized by the preamble itself, is merely a summary of the ancient and traditional law. . . .

This body of law, containing the legal tradition of the Spanish people and also influenced by the Catholic doctrine

---

[102] *Las Siete Partidas*, Ley I, tit. v, part. 4.

[103] Ibid., Ley II.
[104] Ibid., Ley II, tit. xxi, part. 4.
[105] Ibid., Ley III.
[106] *Las Siete Partidas*, Ley VIII.
[120] *Real Cedula de Su Magestad sobre la Educacion, Trato, y Occupaciones de los Esclavos, en Todos sus Dominios de Indias, e Islas Filipinas, Baxo las Reglas que Se Expresan.* This law has been reprinted several times, most recently in an article by Raúl Carrancá y Trujillo in *Revista de Historia de America*, Numero 3 (Mexico, September 1938), pp. 50-9.

of the equality of all men in the sight of God, was biased in favor of freedom and opened the gates to manumission when slavery was transferred to the New World. The law in Spanish and Portuguese America facilitated manumission, the tax-gatherer did not oppose it,[122] and the church ranked it among the works singularly agreeable to God. A hundred social devices narrowed the gap between bondage and liberty, encouraged the master to release his slave, and the bondsman to achieve freedom on his own account. From the sixteenth to the nineteenth century, slaves in Brazil, by reimbursing the original purchase price, could compel their masters to free them.[123] In Cuba and in Mexico the price might be fixed at the request of the Negro, and the slave was freed even if he cost "triple of the sum."[124] The right to have his price declared aided the Negro in seeking a new master, and the owner was required to transfer him to another.[125]

* * *

In effect, slavery under both law and custom had, for all practical purposes, become a contractual arrangement between the master and his bondsman. There may have been no written contract between the two parties, but the state behaved, in effect, as if such a contract did exist, and used its powers to enforce it. This presumed contract was of a strictly limited liability on the part of the slave, and the state, by employing the officially provided protector of slaves, could and did define the financial obligation of the slave to his master in each specific instance as it arose. Slavery had thus from a very early date, at least in so far as the practice was concerned,

moved from a "status," or "caste," "by law of nature," or because of "innate inferiority," or because of the "just judgment and provision of holy script," to become a mere matter of an available sum of money for redemption. Slavery had become a matter of financial competence on the part of the slave, and by that fact lost a great part of the degrading imputation that attached to slavery where it was looked upon as evidence of moral or biological inferiority. Slavery could be wiped out by a fixed purchase price, and therefore the taint of slavery proved neither very deep nor indelible.

In addition to making freedom something obtainable for money, which the slave had the right to acquire and possess, the state made manumission possible for a number of other reasons. A Negro could be freed if unduly punished by his master.[130] He was at liberty to marry a free non-slave (and the master could not legally interfere), and as under the law the children followed the mother, a slave's children born of a free mother were also free.[131] Slaves in Brazil who joined the army to fight in the Paraguayan war were freed by decree on November 6, 1866, and some twenty thousand Negroes were thus liberated.[132] . . .

But significant and varied as were these provisions of the law in the Spanish and Portuguese colonies, they were less important in the long run than the social arrangements and expectancies that prevailed. It was permissible for a slave child in Brazil to be freed at the baptismal font by an offer of twenty milreis,[134] and in Cuba for twenty-five dollars.[135] A female slave could seek a godfather for her baby in some respectable person, hoping that the moral obligation imposed upon the godfather would lead to freeing the child. It was

[122] "In the Cuban market freedom was the only commodity which could be bought untaxed; every negro against whom no one had proved a claim of servitude was deemed free. . . ." William Law Mathieson, op. cit., pp. 37–8.
[123] Sir Harry Johnston, op. cit., p. 89. D. P. Kidder and J. C. Fletcher: *Brazil and the Brazilians* (New York: Childs and Peterson; 1857), p. 133.
[124] Alexander Humboldt: *Political Essay on the Kingdom of New Spain*, translated by John Black (New York: I. Riley; 1811), Vol. I, p. 181.
[125] Richard Henry Dana, Jr.: *To Cuba and Back* (Boston: Tichnor and Fields; 1859), p. 249.

[130] Alexander Humboldt: *Political Essay*, op. cit., p. 181.
[131] Henry Koster: *Travels in Brazil* (Philadelphia: M. Carey & Son; 1817), Vol. II, p. 202. Fernando Ortiz, op. cit., p. 337.
[132] Percy Alvin Martin, op. cit., p. 174.
[134] Robert Southey: *History of Brazil* (London, 1819), Part III, p. 784.
[135] William Law Mathieson, op. cit., p. 37.

both a meritorious and a pious deed to accept such a responsibility and to fulfill its implicit commitments, and it bestowed distinction upon him who accepted them.[136] In the mining regions of Minas Geraes a slave who found a seventeen and a half carat diamond was crowned with a floral wreath, dressed in a white suit, carried on the shoulders of fellow slaves to the presence of his master, and freed and allowed to work for himself.[137] A parent having ten children could claim freedom, whether male or female.

The freeing of one's slaves was an honorific tradition, and men fulfilled it on numerous occasions. Favorite wet nurses were often freed; slaves were manumitted on happy occasions in the family—a birth of a first son, or the marriage of one of the master's children. In fact, the excuses and the occasions were numerous—the passing of an examination in school by the young master, a family festival, a national holiday, and, of course, by will upon the death of the master.[138] A cataloguing of the occasions for manumission in such a country as Brazil might almost lead to wonder at the persistence of slavery; but as I have pointed out above, the importations of slaves were large and continuous in Brazil all through the colonial period and late into the nineteenth century.

Opportunities for escape from slavery were further facilitated by the system of labor that prevailed in many places, particularly in cities. Slaves were often encouraged to hire themselves out and bring their masters a fixed part of their wages, keeping the rest. Skilled artisans, masons, carpenters, blacksmiths, wheelwrights, tailors, and musicians were special gainers from the arrangement.[139] But even ordinary laborers were allowed to organize themselves in gangs, *gente de Ganho*, as they were called.

With all its cruelty, abuse, hardship, and inhumanity, the atmosphere in Brazil and in the Spanish-American countries made for manumission. Even in the rural regions individuals were allowed to sell the products from their own plots, given them to work for themselves, and to save their money toward the day of freedom. In Cuba, one writer notes, the raising of pigs by slaves provided a ready source of the sums accumulated for such a purpose.[143] It should be further noticed that, in addition to their Sundays, the Negroes in Brazil had many holidays, amounting all together to eighty-four days a year, which they could use for their own purposes, and for garnering such funds as their immediate skill and opportunities made possible. The purchase of one's freedom was so accepted a tradition among the Negroes that many a Negro bought the freedom of his wife and children while he himself continued laboring as a slave, and among the freed Negroes societies were organized for pooling resources and collecting funds for the freeing of their brethren still in bondage.[144]

These many provisions favoring manumission were strongly influenced by the church. Without interfering with the institution of slavery where the domestic law accepted it, the church early condemned the slave trade and prohibited Catholics from taking part in it. The prohibition was not effective, though it in some measure may have influenced the Spaniards to a rather limited participation in the trade as such. . . .

The presumption against the slave trade was that it forced people into slavery outside the law and against their will. More important in the long run than the condemnation of the slave trade proved the church's insistence that slave and master were equal in the sight of God. Whatever the formal relations between slave and master, they must both

[136] Henry Koster, op. cit., p. 195.
[137] John Mawe: *Travels in the Interior of Brazil* (London: Longman, Hurst, Rees, Orme & Brown; 1812), p. 318.
[138] Percy Alvin Martin, op. cit., p. 170.
[139] Fernando Ortiz, op. cit., p. 318.

[143] Rev. Abiel Abbot: *Letters Written in the Interior of Cuba* (Boston: Bowles and Dearborn; 1829), p. 97.
[144] Arthur Ramos: *The Negro in Brazil*, translated from the Portuguese by Richard Pattee (Washington, D.C., 1939), p. 70.

recognize their relationship to each other as moral human beings and as brothers in Christ. The master had an obligation to protect the spiritual integrity of the slave, to teach him the Christian religion, to help him achieve the privileges of the sacraments, to guide him into living a good life, and to protect him from mortal sin. The slave had a right to become a Christian, to be baptized, and to be considered a member of the Christian community. . . .

From the very beginning the Catholic churches in America insisted that masters bring their slaves to church to learn the doctrine and participate in the communion. The assembled bishops in Mexico in the year 1555 urged all Spaniards to send the Indians, and especially the Negroes, to church;[147] similarly in Cuba in 1680.[148]

In fact, Negroes were baptized in Angola[149] before leaving for their Atlantic journey to Brazil. Upon arrival they were instructed in the doctrine, and as evidence of their baptism carried about their necks a mark of the royal crown. As a Catholic the slave was married in the church, and the banns were regularly published.[150] It gave the slave's family a moral and religious character unknown in other American slave systems. It became part of the ordinary routine on the slave plantations for the master and slaves to attend church on Sundays, and regularly before retiring at night the slaves gathered before the master's house to receive his blessings.[151] If married by the church, they could not be separated by the master. Religious fraternities sprang up among the slaves. These were often influential and honorific institutions, with regularly elected officers, and funds for the celebration of religious holidays subscribed to by the slaves out of their own meager savings. In Brazil

the slaves adopted the Lady of the Rosary as their own special patroness, sometimes painting her black. In a measure these religious fraternities emulated those of the whites, if they did not compete with them, and the slaves found a source of pride in becoming members, and honor in serving one of these religious fraternities as an official.[152]

If the Latin-American environment was favorable to freedom, the British and American were hostile.[153] Legal obstacles were placed in the way of manumission, and it was discouraged in every other manner. The presumption was in favor of slavery.[154] A Negro who could not prove that he was free was presumed to be a runaway slave and was advertised as such; if no claimant appeared, he was sold at public auction for the public benefit.[155] . . . In most of the British colonies heavy taxes had been imposed on manumission, and as late as 1802 a law was passed in the Northern Leeward Islands requiring the owner who would register his slave for manumission to pay five hundred pounds into the public treasury,[156] and this sum had to be provided in his will if it made provision for the liberation of the slave. . . .

In the southern part of the United States the position of the slave was closely similar to that in the British West Indies. What is important to note is the tendency to identify the Negro with the slave. The mere fact of being a Negro

---

[147] *Concilios Provinciales, Primero y Segundo, Mexico, En los Años de 1555 y 1565* (Mexico, 1769), Concilio primero, Cap. III, p. 44.
[148] José Antonio Saco, op. cit., Tomo I, pp. 165–7.
[149] Henry Koster, op. cit., p. 198.
[150] Ibid., p. 202.
[151] Alfred R. Wallace: *A Narrative of Travels on the Amazon and Rio Negro* (London: Reeve & Co.; 1853), p. 92.

[152] Robert Southey, op. cit., p. 784.
[153] There were, briefly speaking, three slave systems in the Western Hemisphere. The British, American, Dutch, and Danish were at one extreme, and the Spanish and Portuguese at the other. In between these two fell the French. The first of these groups is characterized by the fact that they had no effective slave tradition, no slave law, and that their religious institutions were little concerned about the Negro. At the other extreme there were both a slave law and a belief that the spiritual personality of the slave transcended his slave status. In between them the French suffered from the lack of a slave tradition and slave law, but did have the same religious principles as the Spaniards and Portuguese. If one were forced to arrange these systems of slavery in order of severity, the Dutch would seem to stand as the hardest, the Portuguese as the mildest, and the French, in between, as having elements of both.
[154] Willam Law Mathieson, op. cit., pp. 38–40.
[155] Ibid., pp. 38–40.
[156] Sir Harry Johnston, op. cit., p. 231.

was presumptive of a slave status. South Carolina in 1740 (similarly Georgia and Mississippi) provided that "all negroes, Indians (those now free excepted) . . . mulattoes, or mestizos, who are or shall hereafter be in the province, and all their issue and offspring, born or to be born, shall be and they are hereby declared to be and remain forever hereafter absolute slaves and shall follow the condition of the mother."[158] Equally striking is an early law of Maryland, dating from 1663: "All negroes or other slaves within the province, all negroes to be hereafter imported, shall serve *durante vita*"; and their children were to follow the condition of the father. Significantly the same law said: "That whatsoever free-born women (English) shall intermarry with any slave . . . shall serve the master of such slave during the life of her husband; all the issue of such freeborn women, so married, shall be slave as their fathers were."[159] A free Negro in South Carolina (1740) harboring a runaway slave, or charged "with any criminal matter," upon inability to pay the fine and court charges was to be sold "at public auction."[160] The same state provided that an emancipated Negro set free otherwise than according to the act of 1800 could be seized and kept as a slave by "any person whatsoever."

*   *   *

Because the Negroes were brought in as slaves, the black color raised the presumption of slavery, which was generally extended to mulattoes, and in many states this presumption was enunciated by statute, putting on them the onus of proving that they were free. In Virginia and Kentucky one-fourth Negro blood constituted a presumption of slavery, and all children born of slave mothers were slaves.[163]

Under the British West Indian and United States laws the Negro slave could not hope for self-redemption by purchase, and as slavery was assumed to be perpetual, there was only one route to freedom—manumission. But this route, if not entirely blocked, was made difficult by numerous impediments. The bias in favor of keeping the Negro in servitude contrasts with the other slave systems here under consideration, describes the explicit and the implicit test of the two systems, and foreshadows their ultimate outcome. For the attitude toward manumission is the crucial element in slavery; it implies the judgment of the moral status of the slave, and foreshadows his role in case of freedom.

Just as the favoring of manumission is perhaps the most characteristic and significant feature of the Latin-American slave system, so opposition to manumission and denial of opportunities for it are the primary aspect of slavery in the British West Indies and in the United States. The frequency and ease of manumission, more than any other factor, influence the character and ultimate outcome of the two slave systems in this hemisphere. For the ease of manumission bespeaks, even if only implicitly, a friendly attitude toward the person whose freedom is thus made possible and encouraged, just as the systematic obstruction of manumission implies a complete, if unconscious, attitude of hostility to those whose freedom is opposed or denied. And these contrasting attitudes toward manumission work themselves out in a hundred small, perhaps unnoticed, but significant details in the treatment of the Negro, both as a slave and when freed. Either policy reveals the bent of the system, and casts ahead of itself the long-run consequence of immediate practice and attitude.

*   *   *

The Georgia constitution safeguards against the charge of murder if the "death should happen by accident in giving such slave moderate correction."[174] In South Carolina the act of 1740 pro-

[158] George M. Stroud: *A Sketch of the Laws Relating to Slavery in the Several States of the United States of America* (2nd edition, Philadelphia: H. Longstreth; 1856), pp. 60–1.
[159] Ibid., p. 14.
[160] Ibid., p. 24.
[163] Thomas R. R. Cobb: *An Inquiry into the Law of Negro Slavery in the United States of America* (Philadelphia and Savannah, 1858), p. 238.

[174] Art. 4, par. 12, in ibid., p. 61.

vided that willful murder of a slave should cost the perpetrator "seven hundred pounds current money," and this law, which remained on the statute books till 1821 further provided that if the murder occurred "on sudden heat and passion," it should cost him only £350.[175] But such minor punishments as willfully cutting out the tongue, putting out the eye, castrating, scalding, and similar offenses would, according to the above law, involve the culprit in a cost of merely "one hundred pounds of current money."[176]

Where laws existed protecting the slave against unusual punishment, they were difficult to enforce because he was denied the right to testify in the courts. In the United States, according to Cobb,[177] the rule that slaves could not testify for or against free white persons was enforced without exception; most of the states prohibited such testimony by express statute, others by custom and decision of the courts. In Illinois and Iowa this prohibition extended to free persons of color or emancipated slaves. . . .

The slave had no protector to appeal to, and he could not have his price specified for purposes of redemption and was not allowed to accumulate property to buy his freedom. The slave could acquire no property, and if any property came to him, it would belong to his master;[179] and, being incapable of acquiring property, he could not convey it or give it away. The laws on this point are numerous.

* * *

The marriage contract having no validity, none of its consequences followed. While in a state of slavery, marriage, even with the master's consent, produced no civil effect.[185] . . .

There was no custom of freeing the children at the baptismal font for a nominal price, there was nothing known of the moral role of the godfather for the slave child, and the slave family had no status either in law or in public recognition. . . .

Under the law of most of the Southern states, there was no regard for the Negro family, no question of the right of the owner to sell his slaves separately, and no limitation upon separating husband and wife, or child from its mother. That this was so may be seen from the following advertisements:

NEGROES FOR SALE.—A negro woman, 24 years of age, and her two children, one eight and the other three years old. Said negroes will be sold SEPARATELY or together, *as desired*. The woman is a good seamstress. She will be sold low for cash, or EXCHANGED FOR GROCERIES.
For terms, apply to MATTHEW BLISS & CO., 1 Front Levee

[*New Orleans Bee*]

* * *

"It is a practice, and an increasing practice in parts of Virginia, to rear slaves for market."[199] And the protagonist of slavery Thomas R. Dew, who became president of William and Mary College in 1836, said with pride that "Virginia is in fact a negro raising state for other states; she produces enough for her own supply, and six thousand for sale. . . . Virginians can raise [them] cheaper than they can buy; in fact, it [raising slaves] is one of their greatest sources of profit."[200]

This business had its implications and consequences. The Negro female was reduced to a breeding animal. "She [a girl about twenty years of age] . . . is very prolific in her generating qualities, and affords a rare opportunity for any person who wishes to raise a family of strong, healthy servants for . . . [his] own use. . . ."[201] The emphasis was upon raising children, for they could be sold at high prices. . . . The de-

[175] Ibid., p. 64.
[176] Ibid., p. 66.
[177] Thomas R. R. Cobb, op. cit., p. 230.
[179] Thomas R. R. Cobb, op. cit., p. 238.
[185] Ibid., p. 107.

[199] Quoted in Frederic C. Bancroft, op. cit., p. 69.
[200] Quoted in Frederic C. Bancroft, op. cit., p. 71, from Thomas R. Dew: *Review of the Debate in the Virginia Legislature of 1831 and 1832* (Richmond, 1832).
[201] Quoted by Bancroft, op. cit., p. 74, from the *Charleston Mercury* of May 16, 1838.

mise of the sanctity of marriage had become absolute, and the Negro had lost his moral personality. Legally he was a chattel under the law, and in practice an animal to be bred for the market. The logic of the situation worked itself out in time, but in the process the moral personality of the slave as a human being became completely obscured. It is no wonder that the right of redemption was seemingly nonexistent and the opportunity for manumission greatly restricted.

The contrast between the United States and British West Indian slave law, on the one hand, and the Spanish and Portuguese, on the other, was further heightened by the different role of the church in the life of the Negro. The slaves in the British West Indies were almost completely denied the privileges of Christianity. The plantation-owners opposed the preaching of the gospel on the grounds that it would interfere with the management of the slaves, make them recalcitrant, and put notions of rebellion and freedom into their minds. The argument that the Christian doctrine would make the slaves more obedient, and therefore more docile, found little response among the planters. More surprising than the attitude of the slave-owners is that of the church itself. It is little exaggeration to say, as does one writer on the West Indies, that "The English Church did not recognize them as baptisable human beings."[205] For in spite of the fact that the Society for the Propagation of the Gospel, organized in 1701, declared through the mouth of Bishop Fleetwood, in 1710, that the three hundred Negroes that it had inherited in Barbados had to be brought into the church, and "that if all the slaves in America and every island in those seas were to continue infidels forever, yet ours alone must yet be Christian,"[206] the church remained indifferent to its responsibility. . . .

Nor can it be said that the church in the United States was completely unrestricted in preaching the gospel. A series of regulations governing the assembly of Negroes for worship before dawn or after dark seriously interfered with church gatherings; the outright prohibition of Negro preachers or official frowning upon them, the opposition to acquisition of literacy on the part of either slave or freed man, all combined to restrict the development of a Negro church. And the white church proved incompetent to preach the gospel to all the millions of American Negroes. In South Carolina, in 1800, it was prohibited for "any number" of Negroes, mulattoes, or mestizos, even in company with white persons, to meet together for mental instruction or religious worship "before sunrise or after sunset."[211] Similar laws prevailed in many states.

*   *   *

The contrast, therefore, between the Spanish and Portuguese slave systems on the one hand and that of the British and the United States was very marked, and not merely in their effect upon the slave, but even more significantly upon the place and moral status of the freed man. Under the influence of the law and religion, the social milieu in the Spanish and Portuguese colonies made easy room for the Negroes passing from slavery to freedom. The older Mediterranean tradition of the defense of the slave, combined with the effect of Latin-American experience, had prepared an environment into which the Negro freed from slavery could fit without visible handicap. Slavery itself carried no taint. It was a misfortune that had befallen a human being, and was in itself sufficiently oppressive. The law and religion both frowned upon any attempts to convert this into means of further oppression.

*   *   *

Nothing said above must induce the reader to believe that slavery was anything but cruel. It was often brutal. The

[205] Amos K. Fiske: *The West Indies*, p. 108.
[206] Quoted in the Hon. H. A. Wyndham: *The Atlantic and Slavery*, p. 235.

[211] William Goodell, op. cit., p. 329.

difference between the systems lies in the fact that in the Spanish and Portuguese colonies the cruelties and brutalities were against the law, that they were punishable, and that they were perhaps not so frequent as in the British West Indies and the North American colonies. But these abuses had a remedy at law, and the Negro had a means of escape legally, by compulsory sale if the price were offered, and by many other means. More important was the fact that the road was open to freedom, and, once free, the Negro enjoyed, on the whole, a legal status equal to that of any other subject of the King or to that of any other citizen of the state. And if the question of color was an issue, he could purchase "whiteness" for a specific price.

If we now contrast the position of the freed Negro and people of color in the British possessions with those we have just described, it will become evident that whereas freedom in one place meant moral status, in the other it meant almost the opposite. In the British West Indies the achievement of manumission merely involved a release from the obligation to serve a special master. . . .

The position of the manumitted Negro, or even of the mulatto born of a free mother, was not propitious. The legal and social environment was discriminatory and hostile. The English community opposed manumission, feared the growth of free colored people, and reduced those few who had found a route to freedom to as nearly a servile state as possible. In the United States a very similar policy toward freedmen developed. An act of manumission was merely a withdrawal of the rights of the master. It did not confer citizenship upon the freedmen. That power rested with the state.[224] They were not privileged to bear arms, they had to have a guardian to stand in the relation of a patron to them, and in some instances they were denied the right to purchase slaves as property. They tended to be placed on the same footing as slaves in their contact with whites. . . .

[224] Thomas R. R. Cobb, op. cit., p. 313.

The law, the church, and social policy all conspired to prevent the identification of the liberated Negro with the community. He was to be kept as a separate, a lesser, being. In spite of being manumitted, he was not considered a free moral agent.

The different slave systems, originating under varying auspices, had achieved sharply contrasting results. If we may use such a term, the milieu in Latin America was expansive and the attitude pliable. The Negro may have been racially a new element, but slavery was a known and recognized institution —known especially to the law. The law had long since struggled with the subtleties of freedom and servitude and over a period of centuries had created an elaborate code for the slave, and the new Negro slave was automatically endowed with the immunities contained in the ancient prescription. He was no stranger to the law. His obligation and freedoms within the code were both known. In fact, *the element of human personality was not lost in the transition to slavery from Africa to the Spanish or Portuguese dominions*. He remained a person even while he was a slave. He lost his freedom, but he retained his right to become free again and, with that privilege, the essential elements in moral worth that make freedom a possibility. He was never considered a mere chattel, never defined as unanimated property, and never under the law treated as such. His master never enjoyed the powers of life and death over his body, even though abuses existed and cruelties were performed. Even if justice proved to be blind, the blindness was not incurable. The Negro slave under this system had both a juridical and a moral personality, even while he was in bondage.

This legal tradition and juridical framework were strengthened by the Catholic religion and were part of its doctrine and practice. It made him a member of the Christian community. It imposed upon both the slave and the master equal obligations to respect and protect the moral personality of the other, and for practical purposes it admitted the slave to the privileges of the sacraments. In the mundane world it meant that marriage was a sacred union that could not be broken by mere caprice, that the slave had a right to his wife, and that the slave's family was, like other families, a recognized union in a moral universe, not different from that of his master's family. Here, again, the religious prescriptions were perhaps as often violated as obeyed. But both the state and the church combined to maintain the principle of the rule by the exercise of civil and canon law. The church could and did thunder its opposition to the sins committed against the family—against all Christian families, regardless of color and regardless of status. The church, further, in its emphasis upon the moral equality between master and slave, came to favor manumission and to make it a deed laudable in the sight of God.

The legal right to achieve freedom and the religious favoring of manumission, combined with a number of other features peculiarly American, tended to make easy the path to freedom. That it was easy is seen by the large numbers of freedmen everywhere in Latin America during the colonial period and after independence. . . .

Endowing the slave with a moral personality before emancipation, before he achieved a legal equality, made the transition from slavery to freedom easy, and his incorporation into the free community natural. And as there were always large numbers of freedmen and children of freedmen, it never seemed especially dangerous to increase their number. There was never the question that so agitated people both in the West Indies and in the United States—the danger of emancipation, the lack of fitness for freedom. There was never the horrifying spectacle so often evoked in the United States of admitting a morally inferior and therefore, by implication, a biologically inferior people into the body politic on equal terms.

*   *   *

The different ways in which slavery was finally abolished in the two areas

illumine the social process of which they were an integral part. In the Latin-American area slavery and freedom were, socially and morally speaking, very close to each other. The passage from slavery to freedom was always possible for the individual, and in practice frequent. There was nothing final or inescapable in the slave status. In fact, the contrary was the case. The social structure was malleable, the gap between slavery and freedom narrow and bridgeable, and almost any slave could hope that either he or his family would pass over from his side of the dividing line to the other. Easy manumission all through the period meant that there were always a large number of people in the community who had formerly been slaves and were now free. This is one of the two crucial differences between the character and the outcome of the slave institution in the Latin-American scene on one hand and in the United States on the other. The second basic difference was to be found in the position of the freedman after manumission. In fact, in Latin America there was for legal and practical purposes no separate class of freedmen. The freedman was a free man.[233] In the Latin-American slave system the easy and continuous change of status implied a process of evolution and a capacity for absorption within the social structure that prevented the society from hardening and kept it from becoming divided. We are here face to face with an evolutionary social process that did not allow for a horizontal stratification and favored passage vertically from slavery to freedom. There is, in fact, from this point of view, no slave system; there are only individual slaves. There is no slave by nature, no absolute identification of a given group of individuals as slaves, to whom and to whose children the hope of escape from the hardships they are suffering is forever denied.

If in Latin America the abolition of

[233] There were exceptions to this general statement that could be cited in so large an area and for a period of over three centuries, but both law and practice were bent in the direction of giving the Negro, once freed, a free man's rights.

slavery was achieved in every case without violence, without bloodshed, and without civil war, it is due to the fact that there was no such fixed horizontal division, no such hardening of form that the pattern could no longer change by internal adaptations. In the Latin-American area the principle of growth and change had always been maintained. In the United States the very opposite had come to pass. For reasons of historical accident and conditioning, the Negro became identified with the slave, and the slave with the eternal pariah for whom there could be no escape. The slave could not ordinarily become a free man, and if chance and good fortune conspired to endow him with freedom, he still remained a Negro, and as a Negro, according to the prevailing belief, he carried all of the imputation of the slave inside him. In fact, the Negro was considered a slave by nature, and he could not escape his natural shortcomings even if he managed to evade their legal consequences. Freedom was made difficult of achievement and considered undesirable both for the Negro and for the white man's community in which the Negro resided. The distinction had been drawn in absolute terms, not merely between the slave and the free man, but between the Negro and the white man. The contrast was between color—the Negro was the slave, and the white man was the free man. Attributes of a sharply different moral character were soon attached to these different elements in the population, and they became incompatible with each other. They might as well, so far as the theory was concerned, have been of a different species, for all of the things denied to the Negro as a slave were permitted to the white man—as a citizen. Our Southern slave-holding community had by law and custom, by belief and practice, developed a static institutional ideal, which it proceeded to endow with a high ethical bias.

Marvin Harris

THE ORIGIN OF THE DESCENT RULE

Professor Harris of Columbia University examines the institution of slavery as part of a larger analysis of interracial behavior in the Americas. As an anthropologist, the first question Harris poses is not one of motive or of attitude; rather, he asks what the actual function of racial practices was in both Anglo and Latin America. His analysis suggests that race attitudes followed paths determined by economic roles and that the influence of other cultural forces was marginal in shaping the basic lines of development.

AT one point, and one point only, is there a demonstrable correlation between the laws and behavior, the ideal and the actual, in Tannenbaum's theory: the Spanish and Portuguese codes ideally drew no distinction between the ex-slave and the citizen, and actual behavior followed suit. The large hybrid populations of Latin America were not discriminated against *solely* because they were descended from slaves; it is definitely verifiable that all hybrids were not and are not forced back into a sharply separated Negro group by ap-

Adapted from Marvin Harris, *Patterns of Race in the Americas* (New York, 1964) pp. 79–94. Reprinted by permission of Marvin Harris and Walker and Company.

plication of a rule of descent. This was true during slavery and it was true after slavery. With abolition, because a continuous color spectrum of free men had already existed for at least 200 years, ex-slaves and descendants of slaves were not pitted against whites in the bitter struggle which marks the career of our own Jim Crow.

However, to argue that it was the Spanish and Portuguese slave codes and slave traditions which gave rise to these real and substantial differences in the treatment of the free Negro and mulatto is to miss the essential point about the evolution of the New World plantation systems. If traditional laws and values were alone necessary to get the planters to manumit their slaves, and treat free colored people like human beings, the precedents among the English colonists were surely greater than among the Latins.

If anything, the laws and traditions of England conspired to make its colonists abhor anything that smacked of slavery. And so it was in England that in 1705 Chief Justice Holt could say, "As soon as a Negro comes into England he becomes free." Let it not be forgotten that five of the original thirteen states—New Hampshire, Massachusetts, Connecticut, Rhode Island and Pennsylvania, plus the independent state of Vermont—began programs of complete emancipation before the federal Constitutional Convention met in 1787. Partial anti-slavery measures were enacted by New York in 1788, and total emancipation in 1799, while New Jersey began to pass anti-slavery legislation in 1786. Furthermore, all of the original states which abolished slavery lived up to the declared principles of the Declaration of Independence and the Constitution to a remarkable degree in their treatment of emancipated slaves. "They were citizens of their respective states the same as were Negroes who were free at the time of independence." ...

We see, therefore, that if past laws and values had a significant role to play in the treatment of Negroes and mulattoes, the hounding persecution of the free Negroes and mulattoes should never have occurred in the English colonies. For contrary to the oft-repeated assertion that there was no matrix of English law or tradition into which the slave could fit, it is quite obvious that very specific laws and traditions existed to guide the Anglo-Saxon colonists. These laws and traditions held that all men had natural rights, that the Negroes were men and that slaves ought to become citizens. ...

Understanding of the differences in the status of free "non-whites" in the plantation world can only emerge when one forthrightly inquires why a system which blurred the distinction between Negro and white was materially advantageous to one set of planters, while it was the opposite to another. One can be certain that if it had been materially disadvantageous to the Latin colonists, it would never have been tolerated—Romans, *Siete Partidas* and the Catholic Church notwithstanding. For one thing is clear, the slavocracy in both the Latin and Anglo-Saxon colonies held the whip hand not only over the slaves but over the agents of civil and ecclesiastical authority. To make second-class citizens out of all descendants of slaves was surely no greater task, given sufficient material reason, than to make slaves out of men and brutes out of slaves.

Although the slave plantation per se was remarkably similar in its effects regardless of the cultural background of the slaves or slave-owners the natural, demographic and institutional environment with which slavery articulated and interacted was by no means uniform. It is the obligation of all those who wish to explain the difference between United States and Latin American race relations to examine these material conditions first, before concluding that it was the mystique of the Portuguese or Spanish soul that made the difference.

The first important consideration is demographic. Latin America and the United States experienced totally different patterns of settlement. When Spain and Portugal began their occupation of the New World, they were harassed by severe domestic manpower shortages, which made it extremely difficult for them to find colonists for their far-flung empires. Furthermore, in the New World the conditions under which such colonists were to settle were themselves antithetical to large-scale emigration. In the highlands a dense aboriginal population was already utilizing most of the arable land under the tutleage of the *encomenderos* and *hacendados*. In the lowlands large-scale emigration, supposing there had been a sufficient number of potential settlers, was obstructed by the monopolization of the best coastal lands by the slave-owning sugar planters. Only a handful of Portuguese migrated to Brazil during the sixteenth century. In the seventeenth century, a deliberate policy of *restricting* emigration to Brazil was pursued, out of fear that Portugal was being depopulated. Cried the Jesuit father Antonio Vieira, "Where are our men? Upon every alarm in Alentejo it is necessary to take students from the university, tradesmen from their shops, laborers from the plough!"

The migrations of Englishmen and Britishers to the New World followed an entirely different rhythm. Although the movement began almost a century later, it quickly achieved a magnitude that was to have no parallel in Latin America until the end of the nineteenth century. Between 1509 and 1790 only 150,000 people emigrated from Spain to the entire New World, but between 1600 and 1700, 500,000 English and Britishers moved to the North American territories.

The reason for this accelerated rate of migration is not hard to find:

As opposed to Spain and Portugal, harassed by a permanent manpower scarcity when starting to occupy the Western Hemisphere, seventeenth-century England had an abundant population surplus, owing to the far-reaching changes affecting the country's agriculture since the previous century.

*   *   *

There were plenty of Englishmen eager to settle in the New World but the price of the Atlantic passage was high. The system developed to overcome this obstacle was indentured servitude, whereby the price of passage was advanced, to be worked off, usually in five to eight years, after which the immigrant would be free to do as he might choose. Despite the high mortality rate of the early indentured servants, tens of thousands of Englishmen and women bought passage to the New World in this fashion. The great lure of it was that once a man had worked off his debt, there was a chance to buy land at prices which were unthinkably low in comparison with those of England.

For almost one hundred years, white indentured servants were the principal source of manpower in the Anglo-Saxon colonies. Black slave manpower was a relatively late introduction. The case of Virginia would seem to be the most important and most instructive. In 1624, there were only 22 Negroes in Virginia (at a time when several thousand a year were already pouring into Recife and Bahia). In 1640, they had not increased to more than 150. Nine years later, when Virginia was inhabited by 15,000 whites, there were still only 300 Negroes. It was not until 1670 that Negroes reached 5 per cent of the population. After 1680 slaves began to arrive in increasing numbers, yet it was not until the second quarter of the eighteenth century that they exceeded 25 per cent of the population.

In 1715 the population of all the colonies with the exception of South Carolina was overwhelmingly composed of a white yeomanry, ex-indentured servants and wage earners.

Population of the Colonies, 1715

	WHITE	NEGRO
New Hampshire	9,500	150
Massachusetts	94,000	2,000
Rhode Island	8,500	500
Connecticut	46,000	1,500
New York	27,000	4,000
New Jersey	21,000	1,500
Pennsylvania-Delaware	43,000	2,500
Maryland	40,700	9,500
Virginia	72,000	23,000
North Carolina	7,500	3,700
South Carolina	6,250	10,500

Against a total white population of 375,000, there were less than 60,000 slaves in all of the colonies. If we consider the four Southern colonies—Maryland, Virginia, North Carolina and South Carolina—the ratio was still almost 3 to 1 in favor of the whites.

At about the same time, the total population of Brazil is estimated to have been 300,000, of whom only 100,000 were of European origin. In other words, the ratio of whites to non-whites was the exact opposite of what it was in the United States. A century later (1819) in Brazil, this ratio in favor of non-whites had climbed even higher, for out of an estimated total of 3,618,000 Brazilians, only 834,000 or less than 20 per cent were white. At approximately the same time in the United States (1820), 7,866,797, or more than 80 per cent of the people, out of a total population of 9,638,453 were whites. Although the Negro population was at this time overwhelmingly concentrated in the South, Negroes at no point constituted more than 38 per cent of the population of the Southern states. The high point was reached in 1840; thereafter, the proportion declined steadily until by 1940 it had fallen below 25 per cent in the South and below 10 per cent for the country as a whole.

*   *   *

There is no doubt that the number of Brazilians of color who were free was always greater than the number of free Negroes in the United States, absolutely and in proportion to the number of slaves. But the disparity may not have been as great as many people believe. Thus in 1819, when there were anywhere from 1,500,000 to 2 million slaves in Brazil, there were about 585,000 free men of color (not counting Indians), while in the United States in 1820, 1,538,000 slaves were matched by 233,634 free Negroes. Conservatively, therefore, one might claim that in Brazil there were only about twice as many free Negroes in proportion to slaves as in the United States. This fact permits us to place the claims for a higher rate

of manumission in Brazil in proper perspective and leads us directly to the most important question about the demographic patterns under consideration. The number of free people of color in nineteenth-century Brazil is not at all startling in relationship to the number of *slaves*. What is amazing from the North American point of view is the number of free people of color in relationship to the number of *whites*.

Manumission may have been somewhat more frequent in Brazil than in the United States, but not so much more frequent that one can use it with any certainty as an indication that slavery in Brazil was a milder institution than it was in the United States. It should be borne in mind that the higher ratio of free coloreds to slaves in Brazil might to some extent represent a greater eagerness on the part of Brazilian masters to rid themselves of the care and support of aged and infirm charges. Since we know nothing about the age distribution of the free Brazilian colored population in comparison with that of the United States free colored population, it is obvious that less importance than is customary should be attached to the ratio of free to slave colored in Brazil.

But the ratio of whites to free colored is indeed astonishing, especially if one admits that many of the "whites" quite probably had non-white grandparents. The central question, therefore, is, why did the Brazilian whites permit themselves to become outnumbered by free half-castes? Several factors, none of them related to alleged special features of the Portuguese national character, readily present themselves.

In the first instance, given the chronic labor shortage in sixteenth-century Portugal and the small number of people who migrated to Brazil, the white slaveowners had no choice but to create a class of free half-castes. The reason for this is not that there was a shortage of white women, nor that Porguguese men were fatally attracted to dark females. These hoary sex fantasies explain nothing, since there is no reason why the sexual exploitation of Amerindian and Negro females had necessarily to lead to a *free* class of hybrids. The most probable explanation is that the whites had no choice in the matter. They were compelled to create an intermediate free group of half-castes to stand between them and the slaves because there were certain essential economic and military functions for which slave labor was useless, and for which no whites were available.

One of these functions was that of clearing the Indians from the sugar coast; another was the capture of Indian slaves; a third was the overseeing of Negro slaves; and a fourth was the tracking down of fugitives. The half-caste nature of most of the Indian-fighters and slave-catchers is an indubitable fact of Brazilian history. . . .

[Another] great interstice filled by free half-castes was the cattle industry. The sugar plantations required for the mills and for the hauling of wood and cane, one ox and one horse per slave. These animals could not be raised in the sugar zone, where they were a menace to the unfenced cane fields and where the land was too valuable to be used for pasturage. As a matter of fact, a royal decree of 1701 prohibited cattle raising within 10 leagues of the coast. The cattle industry developed first in the semi-arid portions of the state of Bahia and rapidly fanned out in all directions into the interior. Open-range mounted cowboys, for obvious reasons, cannot be slaves; nor would any self-respecting Portuguese immigrant waste his time rounding up doggies in the middle of a parched wilderness. . . .

It is also at least a reasonable hypothesis that half-castes were used to help supplement the colony's supply of basic food crops. That there was a perennial shortage of food in the colonial cities and on the sugar plantations is well established. . . .

Who then were the food growers of colonial Brazil? Who supplied Bahia, Recife and Rio with food? Although documentary proof is lacking, it would be most surprising if the bulk of the small farmer class did not consist of aged and infirm manumitted slaves, and favorite Negro concubines who with their mulatto offspring had been set up with a bit of marginal land. There was no one to object in Brazil, if after eight years of lash-driven labor, a broken slave was set free and permitted to squat on some fringe of the plantation.

All those interstitial types of military and economic activities which in Brazil could only be initially filled by half-caste free men were performed in the United States by the Southern yeomanry. Because the influx of Africans and the appearance of mulattoes in the United States occurred only *after* a large, intermediate class of whites had already been established, there was in effect no place for the freed slave, be he mulatto or Negro, to go.

It would be wrong, however, to create the impression that the Southern yeomanry, from whence sprang the "rednecks," "crackers" and hillbillies, were capable of intimidating the lords of the Southern plantations. The brutal treatment suffered by the small white farmers as they were driven back to the hills or into the swamps and pine barrens should suffice to set the record straight. If the slave in the South came less and less frequently to be manumitted and if the freedmen were deprived of effective citizenship, and if mulattoes were forced back into the Negro group by the descent rule, it was not because of the sentimental affinity which Southern gentlemen felt for their own "kind." To be sure, there was an intense feeling of racial solidarity among the whites, but nothing could be more in error than to suppose that the racial camaraderie of planter and yeoman was merely the adumbration of some bio-psychological tendency on the part of racially similar people to stick together and hate people who are different. Race prejudice once again explains nothing; such an explanation is precisely what the planters and yeomen came to agree upon, and what the rest of America has been sold for the last 150 years. There were alternate explanations, but these the American people has never permitted itself to learn.

The most remarkable of all the phenomena connected with the "peculiar institution" in the United States is the failure of the non-slaveholding yeomanry and poor whites who constituted three-fourths of all Southerners to destroy the plantation class. These whites were as surely and as permanently the victims of the slave system as were the free half-castes and Negroes and the slaves themselves. Their entire standard of living was depressed by the presence of the slaves. Artisans, farmers and mechanics all found themselves in competition with the kind of labor force it is impossible to undersell—people who work for no wages at all!

*   *   *

However, there were thousands of individuals and even organized groups of Southern yeomen and mechanics who understood that they as much as the Negroes were suffering the effects of slavery. Some of them were able to put the story together with breathtaking insight:

When a journeyman printer *underworks* the usual rates he is considered an enemy to the balance of the fraternity, and is called a *"rat."* Now the slaveholders have *ratted* us with the 180,000 slaves till forbearance longer on our part has become criminal. They have *ratted* us till we are unable to support ourselves with the ordinary comfort of a laborer's life. They have *ratted* us out of the social circle. They have *ratted* us out of the means of making our own schools . . . They have *ratted* us out of the press. They have *ratted* us out of the legislature. . . . Come, if we are not worse than brutish beasts, let us but speak the word, and slavery shall die!

But slavery did not succumb at the hands of those who could most easily have killed it, and who, it would seem, had every reason to want it dead. Instead, the Southern yeomanry followed the planters into a war and bled themselves white in defense of the "property" which was the cause of all their sorrow. Why? Were they so loyal to the owners of the slaves because the measure of their hatred for dark skin and curly hair was so great? They fought because they were prejudiced, but it is no ordinary prejudice that leads a man to kill another over his looks.

It is not surprising that a Negro abolitionist, Frederick Douglass, an ex-slave himself, came so close to the answer, which many Americans, including scholars of high repute, cannot face:

The slaveholders, with a craftiness peculiar to themselves, by encouraging the enmity of the poor, laboring white man against the blacks, succeeded in making the said white man almost as much a slave as the black man himself. The difference between the white slave, and the black slave, is this: the latter belongs to *one* slaveholder, and the former belongs to *all* the slaveholders, collectively. The white slave has taken from him by indirection, what the black slave has taken from him, directly, and without ceremony. Both are plundered, and by the same plunderers. The slave is robbed by his master of all his earnings above what is required for his bare physical necessities; and the white man is robbed by the slave system, of the just results of his labor, because he is flung into competition with a class of laborers who work without wages. . . . At present the slaveholders blind them to this competition by keeping alive their prejudices against the slaves, as *men*—not against them *as slaves*. They appeal to their pride, often denounce emancipation, as tending to place the white working man, on an equality with negroes, and by this means, they succeed in drawing off the minds of the poor whites from the real fact, that, by the rich slave master, they are already regarded as but a single remove from equality with the slave.

This account of the origin of the Southern race mania betrays an understandable tendency to exaggerate both the diabolism of the masters and the stupidity of the poor whites. It does not suffice to account for the equally virulent anti-Negro sentiments in the North as expressed by the Northern mobs which burned Pennsylvania Hall, destroyed the abolitionist presses, burned down a Negro orphan asylum in New York, and rioted against Negroes in almost every major Northern city during the Civil War. It does not explain why the Civil War was begun ostensibly to "save the Union" and why the Emancipation Proclamation could only be sold to the country as a military measure designed to throw additional manpower against the enemy. The fact is, the

Southern planters held a trump. To the abolitionists who warned both the Northern and Southern lower-class farmers and laborers that slavery would eventually drag them all down together, the planters countered that slavery was the only thing that was keeping 4 million African laborers from *immediately* taking the lands, houses and jobs which white men enjoyed. The unleashing of 4 million ex-slaves on the wage market was indeed a nightmare calculated to terrify the poor whites of both regions.

*   *   *

One more point needs to be made before the freed United States Negro and mulatto are properly located in relationship to the immense economic and political forces which were building race relations in their country as they swept the North and South toward civil war. One gains the distinct impression that fear of slave uprisings in the United States was far more pervasive than it was in Brazil, considering the relatively large number of armed whites who confronted the defenseless, brutalized and brainwashed slaves. However, this fear was not based on miscalculation of the enemy. For unlike the case in Brazil, the enemy was not merely the slave, but an organized, vocal, persistent and steadily increasing group of skilled abolitionists who from the very day this country was founded dedicated their lives to the destruction of the slave power. Although Brazil was not entirely devoid of abolitionist sentiment early in the nineteenth century, the scope and intensity of anti-slavery agitation cannot be compared with the furor in the United States. A congressional investigating committee in 1838 was told that there were 1,400 anti-slavery societies in the United States with a membership of between 112,000 and 150,000. In Brazil, the lucky slave fled to a *quilombo*, where cut off from all contact with the rest of the world, the best he could hope for was that the dogs would not find him. In the United States, however, the whole North was a vast *quilombo* in which not only were there escaped slaves but free men of all colors, actively and openly campaigning to bring an end to the thralldom of the whip. The constant patrolling of Southern roads, the fierce punishments for runaways, the laws discouraging manumission, the lumping of free mulattoes with free Negroes, their harassment and persecution and the refusal to permit either of them to reside in some of the slaveholding states, were all part and parcel of the same problem. One wonders what effect it would have had in Brazil, if the larger and more powerful part of the country had been officially dedicated to the proposition that slavery ought to be abolished, and if in every major city in that region freed Negroes and mulattoes had preached and plotted the overthrow of the system. In a sense, the Civil War did not begin in 1860, but in 1776. From the moment this country came into existence the issue of Negro rights was caught in a thousand conflicting currents and countercurrents. Under these circumstances, it hardly seems reasonable to conclude that it is our "Anglo-Saxon Protestant heritage" which is at fault.

Harmannus Hoetink

MASTER-SLAVE RELATIONS AND RACE RELATIONS

NEGRO AND COLOURED

The selections which follow are taken from Hoetink's *The Two Variants in Caribbean Race Relations: A Contribution to the Sociology of Segmented Societies*. In criticizing Tannenbaum, Hoetink's own assumptions become apparent: economic organization is the chief determinant of race relations, and prejudice operates as a dependent variable. Whether or not these assumptions are correct, Hoetink's consideration of American Negro Slavery as part of the Caribbean phenomenon serves a valuable function. It exposes the limitations of studying the American social system from within and employing its traditional conceptions as analytic tools. Professor Hoetink is the Director of the Center for Latin-American Studies at the University of Amsterdam.

MASTER-SLAVE RELATIONS AND RACE RELATIONS

IN investigations of the differences in race relations between the Iberian and North-West European regions of the Caribbean, little attempt seems to have been made to analyse these relations specifically. Nor did the authors I have quoted take particular trouble to observe differences in the groups into which the different races can be divided. This is quite understandable, since the search for general statements necessitates a certain degree of abstraction of a reality which is all too complex. This same social reality, however, forces us to distinguish constantly, in our generalizations, between at least three categories of non-whites: the slave, the Negro, and the mulatto (the 'coloured'). The relations of the white with each of these categories will be discussed below, although no attempt will be made at completeness in the description of these relations. . . .

Tannenbaum considers that the degree of liberality or cruelty in systems of slavery is determined mainly by the favourable or unfavourable influence of religion and law in a society. He goes out of his way to show the legislation of the Latin American areas as recognizing and protecting the moral and legal dignity of the slave, whereas—in his view —the law of the North-West European regions denied this dignity and equated the slave with the chattel. He rightly states that, however important the legal provisions with regard to the slave were in Spanish and Portuguese areas, in the long run they were less decisive than the prevailing 'social arrangements and expectancies' and thus subordinates formal laws and the juridical concept of the slave to the actual practice of social reality. Tannenbaum apparently considers that this subordination applies only to the Latin American area. As soon as he begins to discuss the situation in the south of the United States, he regards the law as more decisive: 'the many thousands of instances of kindness, affection and understanding between master and slave . . . these were personal

From *The Two Variants in Caribbean Race Relations: A Contribution to the Sociology of Segmented Societies* by Harmannus Hoetink, translated by Hookyas, and published by the Oxford University Press for the Institute of Race Relations, 1967, pp. 23–35.

and with no standing in the law. Legally there was no effective remedy against abuse and no channel to freedom.'

Tannenbaum may be criticized not only for this inconsistency but also for his assertion that there was no legal protection for slaves in the southern United States. There was the 'Black Code' of Louisiana of 1806, not quite two decades after the famous Spanish American Code. The Louisiana Code stipulated that, generally, slaves should not be made to work on Sundays; if they did, they had to be paid for their labour. It also prescribed in detail the minimum in food and clothing to which slaves were entitled, and the treatment of sick slaves. It stated that half an hour should be allowed for the morning meal and one and a half hours for that in the afternoon; that disabled slaves might not against their wish be sold without their children, and that children below the age of ten should not be sold separately from their mothers. The Code also laid it down that anybody might lodge a complaint with the court on behalf of a maltreated slave. Justices of the Peace were empowered to obtain information regarding the maltreatment of slaves in their district and to institute legal proceedings when this occurred.

On the other hand, Tannenbaum's enthusiasm for the Brazilian slave laws might be somewhat diminished by the arguments by the contemporary Brazilian scholar Florestan Fernandes. The latter demonstrates that the *Codigo Negro* was not linked to the Constitution, nor to the civil code, and the position of the slave in Brazil was, in fact, marked by his complete *incapacidade civil*. He himself had no right to lodge a complaint with the court, but could do this only through his master or another free citizen; he could not bear witness against his master; he could, in the public interest, be used as an informant, but could not be a sworn witness.

There is no need to mention or analyse further the official directives regarding the treatment of slaves in the Caribbean, for the social reality of the application of these protective laws is far more significant than the laws as such. It is in this respect that Tannenbaum merits most criticism, for he did not sufficiently appreciate the extent to which this reality was affected by economic factors.

Slavery was not exclusively or principally an indication of the cruelty, or liberality, of *race* relations, but above all an economic institution, an 'industrial system,' as Nieboer put it.

The Trinidad sociologist and politician Eric Williams is one of Tannenbaum's fiercest critics. His *Capitalism and Slavery* is written from the economic, determinist point of view, and the evidence and interpretations contradicting Tannenbaum, in this and other of his publications, are considerable. Williams, for instance, draws attention to the cruelty of the plantation system in Haiti in 1789, in sharp contrast with relatively liberal relations between master and slave found in Trinidad at that date. The slave code of Cuba of 1789, he observes, is completely different in its practical application from that of 1840. He continues:

The attempt has been made to explain these divergences as a difference between the Latin tradition and the Anglo-Saxon, between Protestantism and Catholicism. This is far too simple. The explanation is rather to be sought in the nature of property in these different countries at different periods.

For, as he explains, Haiti in 1789 and Cuba in 1840 both had plantation economies producing for a world market, while Cuba and Trinidad in 1789 had largely self-sufficient economies which permitted the existence of 'paternal slavery and benevolent despotism.'

There is much more evidence to support Williams's views. In the same way, Mintz has demonstrated similarities between eighteenth-century Jamaica and nineteenth-century Puerto Rico, where booms in the sugar economy led to increased importation and harsher treatment of slaves. There are also similarities between nineteenth-century Jamaica and eighteenth-century Puerto Rico, where in those periods the economic importance of the plantation was much less....

Not only the treatment of slaves but the rate of manumission, the 'channel to freedom,' was also partly determined by economic factors. A large number of ways in which the slave in Latin America could obtain his freedom, some related to religious factors, are enumerated by Tannenbaum. It would not be difficult to compile a similar list of ways to manumission for the Southern states of the United States. A number of slaves there, as in South America, had gained freedom by performing public services, such as military service during the Revolution. The most common motive for the private manumission of slaves derived from religious scruples; other reasons were also of a 'personal and emotional nature.'

The purchase by slaves of their own freedom and that of members of their family certainly also occurred in the South of the United States. If a slave bought members of his family, but did not comply with manumission formalities, however, these members of his family were officially his slaves. This may explain why in 1860 the number of Negro slave-owners in the United States was estimated at 6,230. The survival of formal master-slave relationships between Negroes and members of their family can be blamed in part on the legal complications through which some of the Southern states in certain periods tried to obstruct manumission. With the exception of Missouri, 'all the states which either countenanced or mildly favored freedom passed laws at a later period restricting it.' There do appear to have been laws encouraging manumission in the Southern states, but they were revoked in the course of the eighteenth and nineteenth centuries, or amended in a spirit contrary to that of the law. It may be surmised that this tendency was to be attributed to the increasing importance of the cotton-plantation economy in the Deep South. The tendency to manumit slaves was certainly strongest in the northern group of the Southern states, where slavery was least profitable. The fact that three-eighths of the free Negroes in 1850 were classified as 'mulattoes,' as compared

with only one-twelfth of the slave population, seems to indicate that the masters preferred to manumit their children by slaves. . . .

Von Humboldt relates how, during his stay in Cuba, he had heard most businesslike discussions of the question whether it was to the master's greater advantage not to make his slaves work too hard, so that they would not need to be replaced too soon, or whether it was more advisable to take out of a slave all one could in a few years and then to replace him with one fresh from Africa. One would, indeed, like to know more about the physical condition of manumitted slaves and their capacity for work. Mortality amongst slaves in Cuba was very high in von Humboldt's time, much higher than in the United States. . . .

One may admit the importance of economic influences on manumission and yet maintain, as Tannenbaum does, that since there were in the Southern United States before Abolition no such great numbers of freedmen as in Brazil or Cuba, the United States Negro had no 'experience in freedom.'

It is difficult to contradict this opinion in view of the vagueness of the expression 'great numbers.' It is undoubtedly true that the United States never witnessed a situation like that in Brazil in 1888, the year in which slavery was abolished, when there were already three times as many free people as there were slaves. A little further back in Brazilian history, however, the figures are more like those from the Deep South. According to a conservative estimate, 3,300,000 slaves were imported into Brazil in the seventeenth and eighteenth centuries. Assuming that natural increase equalled the number of manumissions, so that we may estimate the number of Brazilian slaves at the end of the eighteenth century at some three million, then this number may be compared with the 406,000 freedmen of 1789. The same sort of proportions may be found in the United States, where in 1810 there were 1,191,000 slaves to 186,440 freedmen; in 1830 there were 2,009,000 slaves and as many as 319,-

000 freedmen, or more than 15 per cent. It is worth noting that the Brazilian historian Ianni also reaches the conclusion that, with the exception of the years just before the final abolition of slavery, manumission of slaves was 'on a scale sufficiently modest not to affect the régime.'

If one speaks of 'great numbers' of freedmen only if they outnumber the slaves by 200 per cent, as they did in Brazil around 1880, it should, nevertheless, be noted that at that time slavery had already been abolished in the North-West European areas of the Caribbean. In seeking to verify the supposed liberality of Iberian slave systems by comparing them with conditions in the Iberian peninsula itself, we are confronted with an account (1571) by the Italian Venturino, who remarked that the Portuguese seemed to regard their slaves in the same way as Italians their race horses, and attempted to produce as many of them as possible, in order to sell them for some thirty or forty crowns.

This remark recalls Tannenbaum's view that in the West European areas the slave was classed juridically as 'chattel'; a view which is contradicted by Davie. We may wonder in this connection how it happened that Dutch slave traders, like those in Curaçao, used the Iberian term *picos de India* ('pieces from the Indies') in referring to slaves.

It is doubtful whether much credence should be given to the view advanced by some that in the North-West European areas the concept of the slave was more closely associated with that of the Negro than it was in the Iberian areas. In Spanish, after all, a slave trader was called a *negrero*. And how much value should be attached to the Catholic exhortations against the slave-trade when we learn that in Brazil the Jesuits were involved in trade in Indian slaves? This

they did, it is true, in order to build churches from the profits. Moreover, slave-ownership by Catholic Church functionaries was far from uncommon, even in Protestant-dominated Curaçao. Nor is there any need to repeat Freyre's detailed descriptions of maltreatment of slaves in Brazil (which he regards as expressions of the inevitable sadism of the master in a slave society), in order to reach the following conclusions.

The institution of slavery in the Caribbean concerns the master-slave relationship as well as that of white to Negro: that is to say, economic and juridical subjection coincide with racial subjection. It may be that in comparable economic situations in Iberian society the relations between white master and black slave were friendlier and more supple than in a North-West European Caribbean society, in the same way as, in general, the non-intimate social relationships between races in the Iberian variant are warmer; but this supposition can scarcely be proved. It does, however, seem true that economic factors strongly influence such relations.

As regards manumission, the Catholic Church may be supposed to have provided a greater stimulus in this respect than Protestantism; there is no doubt, however, that economic factors also played a part. In view of the demonstrable significance of economic factors, there is no justification for adducing the 'cruelty' or 'liberality' of any given system of slavery, nor the frequency of manumission, as indications of the nature of the *race* relations as such in the society in which this system of slavery operates. We may conclude that comparisons between conditions of slavery in the two Caribbean variants have proved to be of little relevance in the investigation of differences in 'race relations' *per se*.

NEGRO AND COLOURED

According to Tannenbaum there were Negro priests and even 'black bishops' in Brazil as early as the eighteenth century. Once freed, the Negro in Brazil experienced no obstacles on his way to 'incorporation into the community, in so far as his skills and abilities made that possible.' Tannenbaum's picture of the freed Negro in Brazil suggests his complete social acceptance by the rest of society and his integration in its institutions; in this context one should remember that in Tannenbaum's opinion the freedmen in the Southern United States were not only very few in number before the abolition of slavery, but were also deprived of all 'moral acceptance' and chances of social rise.

It may be relevant here to examine the comments on the social position of the freedmen in Brazil at the beginning of the nineteenth century by Henry Koster, a traveller in that country. To begin with, Koster remarks that European notions of superiority had not been entirely abandoned, and in certain ordinances whites had preferential rights. Thus, whites could be condemned to death only in some places. 'People of colour' were not eligible for certain of the higher official posts, nor were they admitted to the priesthood. The people of mixed race, however, took considerable advantage of liberal interpretations of the law. Local laws and regulations to their disadvantage had mostly become obsolete; mulattoes were admitted to religious orders, and a mulatto could be appointed as a magistrate. On such occasions their personal papers recorded them as white. When Koster inquired once whether a certain *Capitão-mor* was not really a mulatto, the answer was: *'Era, porem ja nâm he'*: 'Yes, he was, but he is not any longer.' When he asked for further elucidation, the reply was: 'How could a *Capitão-mor* possibly be a mulatto?' Several priests also appeared to show signs of Negro ancestry.

There existed special mulatto regiments which did not accept any whites in their ranks. In the white regiments, whose officers had officially to be white, in actual practice one saw 'rather reputed white men,' for no special trouble was taken to investigate whether these officers were not of mixed race. The 'regiments of the line' admitted all except Negroes and Indians. The officers of these regiments had to belong to the nobility. Some of the racially mixed families in Brazil had titles and their members were thus to be found as regimental officers.

Marriages between white men and 'women of colour' were far from rare, although sufficiently noticeable to cause comment. Such comment, however, 'is only made if the person is a planter of any importance, and the woman is decidedly of dark colour, for even a considerable tinge will pass for white. If the white man belongs to the lower orders, the woman is not accounted as being unequal to him in rank, unless she is nearly black.' Marriages between poor Europeans and daughters of well-to-do coloured families were frequent. Wealthy Brazilians of the highest class, however, did not favour marriages with persons whose mixed descent was 'very apparent.' Relationships with such persons usually took the form of a long-standing liaison.

So far we have considered some of Koster's comments on the 'free coloureds.' He continues with the social position of the 'Creole Negroes,' the free Negroes who had been born in the country and who, being of African descent, made no claim to be racially mixed. The very impossibility of being mistaken for members of 'any other caste,' linked them closely together. The free Creole Negroes, like the coloureds and the whites, had their own regiments with their own Negro officers. Some whites made fun of these well-uniformed officers behind their backs, probably, according to Koster, because their display of badges of rank hurt European feelings of superiority.

The Creole Negroes of Recife were mostly artisans; they had not yet reached the higher echelons of social life 'as gentlemen, as planters, as merchants.' Some of them had amassed considerable fortunes and owned many slaves to whom they taught their own trade and from whom they derived great financial benefit. The best church painter of Pernambuco was a black man, with good manners 'and quite the air of a man of some importance though he does not by any means assume too much.' The Negroes were excluded from the priesthood and all official positions which the mulattoes, thanks to liberal application of the law, were able to obtain but 'which the decided and unequivocal colour of the Negro entirely precludes him from aspiring to.' Nor could Negroes join the guard regiments, which, Koster remarks, also prevented them from being maltreated in such units.

The men whose task it was to trace runaway slaves were virtually all freed Negroes; bold men who returned these slaves to their lawful owners, usually with the aid of two or three dogs who sometimes had to tackle and throw the runaway.

It may be noted that Koster painstakingly maintains the distinction between free Negroes and free coloureds, their position and their chances of promotion in Brazilian society—a distinction which is ignored by a modern author like Tannenbaum. Tannenbaum not only extends the supposedly greater liberality of slavery in Spanish America to the essentially different sphere of race relations, but also tends to regard evidence about the social position of Brazilian coloured as valid also in respect of the Brazilian free Negro. He tends to identify the two groups, and in his book the word 'Negro' is used most frequently, while he uses 'mulatto' only incidentally, to add force to his argument: that 'the Negro, especially the mulatto' occupied a more favourable position in Brazil than in the United States. For Tannenbaum, then, the mulatto is a special kind of Negro. Thus, Tannenbaum applies the North American concept of 'Negro' to the Brazilian situation: that is to say that North American standards (by which anyone who is known to have a certain amount of Negro 'blood' in his veins is regarded as a Negro and treated accordingly by the white man) are applied in the evaluation of a society in which wholly different standards were (and are) valid, and where the distinction between Negro and coloured had (and has) considerable social significance, as is demonstrated by Koster's picture of social reality. It seems curiously paradoxical that an investigator like Tannenbaum, whose moral concern

about the race problem in his own country is evident from his publications, finds it so difficult to detach himself from the standards of his own society and applies them uncritically to other societies.

Tannenbaum is not the only North American whose evaluation of the race problem in other societies is clouded by this conceptual self-delusion. Cahnman remarked, with reference to Pierson's *Negroes in Brazil*, that this book 'stands for a type of literature on South America which is most revealing if read between the lines. It reveals that the main practical difference between Anglo-American and Latin-American race-attitudes is in the position of the Mulatto rather than the Negro.' Indeed, this fusion of the two concepts 'Negro' and 'coloured' into one, 'Negro,' which is then, incidentally, analysed into its special components, makes it necessary to read between the lines in order to achieve any real distinction between the Latin and North-West European variants.

As an incidental comment on Tannenbaum's assertion of the liberal attitude of Church and State to admission of Negroes to the priesthood in the Latin American areas, it should be noted that Portuguese laws also denied Moors and Negroes entry to the priesthood, while in Puerto Rico the Negro was excluded from various Government functions as well as from the priesthood.

In the French Caribbean, racial divisions existed physically inside the Churches. With reference to eighteenth-century Martinique, Rennard writes that within the church building there was *'une démarcation tres nette,'* which separated the whites from the coloureds, Negroes and slaves. *'Les gens de couleur ne pouvaient occuper que les derniers bancs; ils ne pouvaient avoir que la dernière classe dans les cérémonies faites en leur faveur.'* In the cemetery the free were buried separately from the slaves, and sometimes the whites from the others. It is clear that even in consecrated places the reality could be far removed from the professed equality before God. . . .

David B. Davis

THE CONTINUING CONTRADICTION OF SLAVERY:

A COMPARISON OF BRITISH AMERICA AND LATIN AMERICA

In 1966 David Brion Davis's *The Problem of Slavery in Western Culture* won a Pulitzer Prize for its profound examination of the history of the concept of slavery in Western Europe and its colonies. The selection which follows challenges the argument that cultural factors made slavery milder in Latin America than in Anglo-America, and Davis describes the wide variety of practices found under the heading "slavery." Professor Davis teaches at Yale University.

AS a result of differences in economy, social and political institutions, and the ratio of Negroes to whites, the actual status and condition of colonial slaves varied considerably from one region to another. Yet no slave colony had a monopoly on either kindness or cruelty. Slave codes were often enacted with a view to quieting local fears or appeasing a church or government. Travelers were sometimes biased or quick to generalize from a few fleeting impressions. Since we still seriously lack a thorough comparative study of Negro slavery in the various colonies, we must be content with fragmentary evidence and with extremely tentative conclusions. There would seem to be some basis, however, for questioning two assumptions which have been widely accepted by modern historians.

The first is that Negro slavery in the British colonies and Southern United States was of a nearly uniform severity, the slave being legally deprived of all rights of person, property, and family, and subjected to the will of his owner and the police power of the state, which barred his way to education, free movement, or emancipation. The second assumption is that the French, and especially the Spanish and Portuguese, were far more liberal in their treatment of slaves, whom they considered as human beings who had merely lost a portion of their external freedom. Untainted by racial prejudice and free from the pressures of a fluid, capitalistic economy, these easygoing colonists are supposed to have protected the human rights of the slave and to have facilitated his manumission. Some historians have simply held that slavery in North America was much harsher than that in Latin America, but Stanley M. Elkins has argued more persuasively that the great contrast was not in the bondsman's physical well-being but in the recognition of his basic humanity. As a methodological device, this distinction has obvious merit, since a master might look upon his slaves as subhuman animals and still provide them with comfortable maintenance. On the other hand, it would be unrealistic to draw too sharp a line between moral status and physical treatment. It is difficult to see how a society could have much respect for the value of slaves as human personalities if it sanctioned their torture and

From David B. Davis, *Problem of Slavery in Western Culture* (Ithaca, 1966) pp. 223–243. Reprinted by permission of Cornell University Press.

multilation, the selling of their small children, the unmitigated exploitation of their labor, and the drastic shortening of their lives through overwork and inadequate nourishment. While a few isolated instances of sadistic cruelty would reveal little about the legal or moral status of slaves, we should not exclude physical treatment when it is part of a pattern of systematic oppression which is fully sanctioned by the laws and customs of a society. We shall find, however, that there is other evidence than physical treatment for challenging the assumption that Latin Americans were more sensitive than Anglo-Americans to the essential humanity of their slaves.

*   *   *

A word of explanation is in order regarding the chronological range of selected examples and illustrations. If we are to judge the influence of traditional Catholic culture, the crucial period in Latin American slavery is the early colonial era, before the full impact of the Enlightenment, the American and French Revolutions, and the wars of independence. But when we test the assumption that slavery in the British colonies and Southern United States was of a monolithic character, unmitigated by any recognition of the Negro's rights of personality, it is appropriate to select examples from the nineteenth century, when laws and customs had hardened to form a self-contained system of values and precedents. If some of the ameliorative elements we usually associate with Latin American slavery were common in North America, even at a time when bondage had grown more formalized and severe, then we should have less reason to suppose that the basic evils of the institution could have been eliminated by mere palliative reforms.

By the late eighteenth century most travelers agreed that in Brazil and the Spanish colonies the condition of slaves was considerably better than in British America. Any comparison must consider Negro slavery as a system of forced labor, of social organization, and of class and racial discipline. Numerous accounts from the late eighteenth and nineteenth centuries tell us that the Latin American slave enjoyed frequent hours of leisure and was seldom subjected to the factory-like regimentation that characterized the capitalistic plantations of the north; that he faced no legal bars to marriage, education, or eventual freedom; that he was legally protected from cruelty and oppression, and was not stigmatized on account of his race. This relative felicity has quite plausibly been attributed to a culture that de-emphasized the pursuit of private profit, to the Catholic Church's insistence on the slave's right to marry and worship, and to what Gilberto Freyre has termed the "miscibility" of the Portuguese, which submerged sensitivity to racial difference in a frank acceptance of sexual desire.

No doubt there is much truth in even the idyllic picture of the Brazilian "Big House," where slaves and freemen pray and loaf together, and where masters shrug their shoulders at account books and prefer to frolic with slave girls in shaded hammocks. But we should not forget that West Indian and North American planters were fond of idealizing their own "Big Houses" as patriarchal manors, of portraying their Negroes as carefree and indolent, and of proudly displaying humane slave laws which they knew to be unenforceable. Their propaganda, which was supported by travelers' accounts and which long seemed persuasive to many Northerners and Englishmen, has largely been discredited by numerous critical studies based on a wealth of surviving evidence. Many of the records of Brazilian slavery were destroyed in the 1890's, in a fit of abolitionist enthusiasm, and the subject has never received the careful scrutiny it deserves. Only in recent years have such historians as Octávio Ianni, Fernando Henrique Cardoso, Jaime Jaramillo Uribe, and C. R. Boxer begun to challenge the stereotyped images of mild servitude and racial harmony.

There is little reason to doubt that slavery in Latin America, compared with that in North America, was less subject to the pressures of competitive capitalism and was closer to a system of patriarchal rights and semifeudalistic services. But after granting this, we must recognize the inadequacy of thinking in terms of idealized models of patriarchal and capitalistic societies. Presumably, an exploitive, capitalistic form of servitude could not exist within a patriarchal society. The lord of a manor, unlike the entrepreneur who might play the role of lord of a manor, would be incapable of treating men as mere units of labor in a speculative enterprise. But neither would he think of exploring new lands, discovering gold mines, or developing new plantations for the production of sugar and coffee. It is perhaps significant that accounts of Latin American slavery often picture the relaxed life on sugar plantations after their decline in economic importance, and ignore conditions that prevailed during the Brazilian sugar boom of the seventeenth century, the mining boom of the early eighteenth century, and the coffee boom of the nineteenth century. Similarly, Southern apologists tended to overlook the human effects of high-pressure agriculture in the Southwest, and focus their attention on the easygoing and semipatriarchal societies of tidewater Maryland and Virginia. Eugene D. Genovese has recently suggested that while the North American slave system was stimulated and exploited by the capitalist world market, it retained many precapitalistic features, such as a lack of innovation, restricted markets, and low productivity of labor, and actually gravitated toward an uneconomical paternalism that was basically antithetical to capitalistic values.

Although a particular instance of oppression or well-being can always be dismissed as an exception, it is important to know what range of variation a system permitted. If an exploitive, capitalistic form of servitude was a times common in Brazil and Spanish America, and if North Americans conformed at times to a paternalistic model and openly acknowledged the humanity of their slaves, it may be that differences between slavery in Latin America and the United States were no greater than regional or temporal differences within the countries themselves. And such a conclusion would lead us to suspect that Negro bondage was a single phenomenon, or *Gestalt,* whose variations were less significant than underlying patterns of unity.

Simon Gray, a Natchez river boatman, provides us with an example of the flexibility of the North American slave system. During the 1850's most Southern states tightened their laws and to all appearances erected an impassable barrier between the worlds of slave and freeman. But the intent of legislators was often offset by powerful forces of economic interest and personality. Simon Gray was an intelligent slave whose superior abilities were recognized by both his master and the lumber company which hired his services. In the 1850's this lowly slave became the captain of a flatboat on the Mississippi, supervising and paying wages to a crew that included white men. In defiance of law, Gray was permitted to carry firearms, to travel freely on his own, to build and run sawmills, and to conduct commercial transactions as his company's agent. Entrusted with large sums of money for business purposes, Gray also drew a regular salary, rented a house where his family lived in privacy, and took a vacation to Hot Springs, Arkansas, when his health declined. Although there is evidence that in Southern industry and commerce such privileges were not as uncommon as has been assumed, we may be sure that Simon Gray was a very exceptional slave. He might well have been less exceptional in Cuba or Brazil. The essential point, however, is that regardless of restrictive laws, the Southern slave system had room for a few Simon Grays. The flatboat captain could not have acted as he did if the society had demanded a rigorous enforcement of the law.

By the time Simon Gray was beginning to enjoy relative freedom, Portugal and Brazil were the only civilized nations that openly resisted attempts to suppress the African slave trade. It has been estimated that by 1853 Britain had paid Portugal some £2,850,965 in bribes intended to stop a commerce whose horrors had multiplied as a result of efforts to escape detection and capture. But despite British bribes and seizures, the trade continued, and was countenanced by the society which has been most praised for its humane treatment of slaves. One of the boats captured by the British, in 1842, was a tiny vessel of eighteen tons, whose crew consisted of six Portuguese. Between decks, in a space only eighteen inches high, they had intended to stow two hundred and fifty African children of about seven years of age. Suspicion of Britain's motives probably prevented more outspoken attacks on a trade that outraged most of the civilized world. But the fact remains that Brazilian society not only permtted the slave trade to continue for nearly half a century after it had been outlawed by Britain and the United States, but provided a flourishing market for Negroes fresh from Africa. During the 1830's Brazil imported more than 400,000 slaves; in the single year of 1848 the nation absorbed some sixty thousand more. That the reception of these newcomers was not so humane as might be imagined is suggested by a law of 1869, six years after Lincoln's Emancipation Proclamation, which forbade the separate sale of husband and wife, or of children under fifteen. Not long before, even children under ten had been separated from their parents and sent to the coffee plantations of the south.

These examples are intended only to illustrate the range of variation that could occur in any slave society, and hence the difficulties in comparing the relative severity of slave systems.

*   *   *

In the newly developed lands of captured or ceded colonies, such as Berbice, Demerara, Trinidad, and Louisiana, there were few effective checks on the speculative planter bent on reaping maximum profit in the shortest possible time. And whereas the North American slave frequently lived in a land of peace and plentiful food, his West Indian brother was the first to feel the pinch of famine when war cut off essential supplies, or when his master was burdened by debt and declining profits. On the small tobacco farms of colonial Virginia and Maryland the physical condition of slaves was surely better than in the mines of Minas Gerais or on the great plantations of Bahia, where a Capuchin missionary was told in 1682 that a Negro who endured for seven years was considered to have lived very long.

North American planters were fond of comparing the fertility of their own slaves with the high mortality and low birth rate of those in the West Indies and Latin America, and of concluding that theirs was the milder and more humane system. Such reasoning failed to take account of the low proportion of female slaves in the West Indies, the communicable diseases transmitted by the African trade, and the high incidence of tetanus and other maladies that were particularly lethal to infants in the Caribbean. No doubt differences in sanitation and nutrition, rather than in physical treatment, explain the fact that while Brazil and the United States each entered the nineteenth century with about a million slaves, and subsequent importations into Brazil were three times greater than those into the United States, by the Civil War there were nearly four million slaves in the United States and only one and one-half million in Brazil. But after all such allowances are made, it still seems probable that planters in Brazil and the West Indies, who were totally dependent on fresh supplies of labor from Africa, were less sensitive than North Americans to the value of human life. When a slave's life expectancy was a few years at most, and when each slave could easily be replaced, there was little incentive to improve conditions or limit hours of work.

According to both C. R. Boxer and Celso Furtado, Brazilian sugar planters took a short-term view of their labor needs, and accepted the axiom, which spread to the British Caribbean, that it was good economy to work one's slaves to death and then purchase more. In colonial Brazil, Jesuit priests felt it necessary to admonish overseers not to kick pregnant women in the stomach or beat them with clubs, since this brought a considerable loss in slave property.

But what of the benevolent laws of Latin America which allowed a slave to marry, to seek relief from a cruel master, and even to purchase his own freedom? It must be confessed that on this crucial subject historians have been overly quick to believe what travelers passed on from conversations with slaveholders, and to make glowing generalizations on the basis of one-sided evidence.

Much has been made of the fact that the Spanish model law, *las Siete Partidas*, recognized freedom as man's natural state, and granted the slave certain legal protections. But the argument loses some of its point when we learn that the same principles were accepted in North American law, and that *las Siete Partidas* not only made the person and possessions of the bondsman totally subject to his master's will, but even gave owners the right to kill their slaves in certain circumstances. Some of the early Spanish and Portuguese legislation protecting Indians has erroneously been thought to have extended to Negroes as well. In actuality, the first laws pertaining to Negroes in such colonies as Chile, Panama, and New Granada were designed to prohibit them from carrying arms, from moving about at night, and above all, from fraternizing with Indians. It is true that in the late seventeenth and early eighteenth centuries the Portuguese crown issued edicts intended to prevent the gross mistreatment of Negro slaves. But as C. R. Boxer has pointed out, Brazilian law was a chaotic tangle of Manueline and Filipine codes, encrusted by numerous decrees which often contradicted one another, and which were interpreted by lawyers and magistrates notorious for their dishonesty. Even if this had not been true, slaves were dispersed over immense areas where there were few towns and where justice was administered by local magnates whose power lay in land and slaves. It is not surprising that in one of the few recorded cases of the Portuguese crown intervening to investigate the torture of a slave, nothing was done to the accused owner. This revisionist view receives support from Jaime Jaramillo Uribe's conclusion that the judicial system of New Granada was so ineffective that even the reform legislation of the late eighteenth century did little to change the oppressive life of Negro slaves.

In theory, of course, the Portuguese or Spanish slave possessed an immortal soul that entitled him to respect as a human personality. But though perfunctorily baptized in Angola or on the Guinea coast, he was appraised and sold like any merchandise upon his arrival in America. Often slaves were herded in mass, stark naked, into large warehouses where they were examined and marketed like animals. As late as the mid-nineteenth century the spread of disease among newly arrived Negroes who were crowded into the warehouses of Rio de Janeiro brought widespread fears of epidemic. The Spanish, who ordinarily sold horses and cows individually, purchased Negroes in lots, or *piezas de Indias*, which were sorted according to age and size. There is abundant evidence that Brazilians were little troubled by the separation of Negro families; in the 1850's coffee planters in the rich Parahyba Valley thought nothing of selling their own illegitimate children to passing traders. Despite protests from priests and governors, it was also common practice for Brazilians to purchase attractive girls who could profitably be let out as prostitutes.

In Brazil, as in other slave societies, there were apparently authentic reports of bondsmen being boiled alive, roasted in furnaces, or subjected to other fiendish punishments. More significant than such extreme cases of sadism is the evidence that planters who were successful and were accepted as social leaders equipped their estates with the chambers and instruments of torture; that it was common custom to punish a recalcitrant slave with *novenas,* which meant that he would be tied down and flogged for nine to thirteen consecutive nights, his cuts sometimes being teased with a razor and rubbed with salt and urine. In the mid-eighteenth century, Manuel Ribeiro Rocha attacked the Brazilian "rural theology" which allowed masters to welcome their new slaves with a vicious whipping, to work them in the fields without rest, and to inflict one hundred or more lashes without cause. A century later planters in the Parahyba Valley taught their sons that Negroes were not true men but inferior beings who could only be controlled by continued punishment; and some of the clergy maintained that Africans were the condemned sons of Cain. This widespread conviction of racial inferiority justified a regime of hatred and brutality in which the slave had no right of appeal and even fatal beatings went unpunished.

Obviously much depended on regional differences in economy and social tradition. The recent studies of the extreme southern provinces of Brazil by Octávio Ianni and Fernando Cardoso reveal a picture of harsh chattel slavery and racial prejudice which stands in marked contrast to the familiar images of benign servitude in the north. During the last third of the eighteenth century the southern states developed a capitalistic economy which was initially stimulated by the export of wheat but which came to rely heavily on the production of jerked beef. Whether engaged in agriculture, stock raising, or the processing of meat or leather, the slaveholding capitalists were bent on maximizing production for commercial profit. Because the economy rested on slave labor and because physical labor was largely associated with the African race, Negroes and mulattoes were regarded as mere instruments of production, wholly lacking in human personality. According to Ianni, the slave was a totally alienated being; able to express himself only through the intermediary of his owner, he was under the complete dominion of a master class which rigidly controlled his movements and held power over his life and death. Though kind and paternalistic masters were to be found in Paraná, Santa Catarina, and Rio Grande do Sul, as elsewhere in the Americas, the overriding fact is that the ideology and judicial framework of southern Brazil were geared to the maintenance of an exploitive system of labor, to the preservation of public security, and to the perpetuation of power in the hands of a white ruling caste. At every point the Negro was forced to shape his behavior in accordance with the actions and expectations of the white man.

Conditions were undoubtedly better in the cities, where protective laws were more often enforced and where Negroes had at least a chance of acquiring money that could purchase freedom. But in colonial Cartagena, Negro slaves were subject to the most repressive police regulations, and to punishments which ranged from death to the cutting off of hands, ears, or the penis. In Mariana the city councilors demanded in 1755 that the right to purchase freedom be withdrawn and that slaves who tried to escape be crippled for life. While both the proposals aroused the indignation of the viceroy at Bahia, they indicate the state of mind of a master class which, in Minas Gerais, posted the heads of fugitive slaves along the roadsides. And men who accepted such brutality as a necessary part of life could not always be expected to abandon their fields or shut down their sugar mills on thirty-five religious holidays, in addition to fifty-two Sundays. It was not an idyllic, semifeudal servitude that made colonial Brazil widely known as "the hell for Negroes," and as a place where their lives would be "nasty, brutish, and short"; or that drove countless bondsmen to suicide or revolt, and reduced others to a state of psychic shock, of flat apathy and depression, which was common enough in Brazil to acquire the special name of *banzo*.*

*   *   *

In conclusion, it would appear that the image of the warmly human Big House must be balanced by a counter-image of the brutal society of the coffee barons, who even in the 1870's and 1880's governed a world in which there were no gradations between slavery and freedom. In their deep-rooted racial prejudice, their military-like discipline, their bitter resistance to any restrictions on a slaveowner's will, their constant fear of insurrection, and their hostility toward meaningful religious instruction of their Negroes, these planters were hardly superior to their brothers in Mississippi. Even with the approach of in-

---

* Boxer, *Golden Age of Brazil*, pp. 7–9; Boxer, *Race Relations in Portuguese Colonial Empire*, p. 101; Stein, *Vassouras*, pp. 139–41; Pierson, *Negroes in Brazil*, pp. 3–7; Ramos, *Negro in Brazil*, p. 36. It is interesting to note that, according to Elkins, slavery in the United States was so severe and absolute that it molded the Negro's character into a submissive, childlike "Sambo," whose traits resembled those of the victims of Nazi concentration camps. Elkins could find no "Sambos" in Latin America, and concludes that the character type was unique to the United States (*Slavery*, pp. 81–139). Without debating the merits of this intriguing thesis, we should point out that one source of "Sambo," which Elkins ignores, can be found in eighteenth-century English literature. In Chapter Fifteen we shall consider how this fictional stereotype suited the tastes of a sentimental age. In actuality, ship captains and planters of various nationalities agreed that when Negroes were subjected to the harshest treatment, their usual responses were revolt, suicide, flight, or a sullen withdrawal and mental depression. The state which the Portuguese described as *banzo* was clearly the result of severe shock which altered the entire personality.

evitable emancipation, they made no effort to prepare their slaves for freedom. It was in the face of this "slave power" that the Brazilian abolitionists resorted to the familiar demands for "immediate" and "unconditional" emancipation, and modeled themselves on the champions of British and American reform. Joaquim Nabuco, the great leader of the Brazilian antislavery movement, adopted the pen name of "Garrison."

With the exception of legal barriers to manumission, . . . the salient traits of North American slavery were to be found among the Spanish and Portuguese. Notwithstanding variations within every colony as a result of environment, economic conditions, social institutions, and the personality of owners, the Negro was everywhere a mobile and transferable possession whose labor and well-being were controlled by another man. Any comparison of slavery in North and South America should take account of the fact that Brazil alone had an area and variety comparable to all British America, and that the privileged artisans, porters, and domestic servants of colonial Brazilian cities can be compared only with their counterparts in New York and Philadelphia. Similarly, conditions in nineteenth-century Alabama and Mississippi must be held against those in the interior coffee-growing areas of south-central Brazil. Given the lack of detailed statistical information, we can only conclude that the subject is too complex and the evidence too contradictory for us to assume that the treatment of slaves was substantially better in Latin America than in the British colonies, taken as a whole.

Stanley M. Elkins

THE DYNAMICS OF UNOPPOSED CAPITALISM

SLAVERY IN CAPITALIST AND NON-CAPITALIST CULTURES

Though Professor Elkins accepts Tannenbaum's distinction between Anglo and Latin American slavery, he sees capitalism as the key to American Negro chattel slavery. In his opinion capitalist values—the exploitative values of individual profit seeking—shaped the fundamental character of Southern society. Elkins' analysis implies a general criticism of the impact of American capitalism on social values. He believes that the slave South was more capitalistic than the North, and that plantation slavery was the natural consequence of applying capitalist principles to agricultural production.

THE DYNAMICS OF UNOPPOSED CAPITALISM

BEFORE reviewing in greater detail the legal aspects of this servitude, we should note that the most vital facts about its inception remain quite unaccounted for. The reasons for its delay have been satisfactorily explained—but why did it occur at all? Why should the drive to establish such a status have got under way when it did? What was the force behind it, especially in view of the prior absence of any sort of laws defining slavery? We may on the one hand point out the lack of any legal structure automatically compelling the Negro to become a slave, but it is only fair, on the other, to note that there was equally little in the form of such a structure to prevent him from becoming one. It is not enough to indicate the simple process whereby the interests of white servants and black were systematically driven apart: what was its dynamic? Why should the status of "slave" have been elaborated, in little more than two generations following its initial definition, with such utter logic and completeness to make American slavery unique among all such systems known to civilization?

Was it the "motive of gain"? Yes, but with a difference. The motive of gain,

as a psychic "fact," can tell us little about what makes men behave as they do; the medieval peasant himself, with his virtually marketless economy, was hardly free from it. But in the emergent agricultural capitalism of colonial Virginia we may already make out a mode of economic organization which was taking on a purity of form never yet seen, and the difference lay in the fact that here a growing system of large-scale staple production for profit was free to develop in a society where no prior traditional institutions, with competing claims of their own, might interpose at any of a dozen points with sufficient power to retard or modify its progress. What happens when such energy meets no limits?

Here, even it its embryonic stages, it is possible to see the process whereby capitalism would emerge as the principal dynamic force in American society. The New World had been discovered and exploited by a European civilization which had always, in contrast with other world cultures, placed a particularly high premium on personal achievement, and it was to be the special genius of Englishmen, from Elizabeth's time onward, to transform this career concept from its earlier chivalric form into one of economic fulfilment—from "glory" to "success." Virginia was settled during the very key period in which the English middle class forcibly reduced, by revolution, the power of those standing institutions—the church and the crown—which most directly symbolized society's traditional limitations upon personal success and mobility. What the return of the crown betokened in 1660 was not so much "reaction" as the fact that all society had by then somehow made terms with the Puritan Revolution. Virginia had proven a uniquely appropriate theater for the acting-out of this narrower, essentially modern ideal of personal, of *economic,* success. Land in the early days was cheap and plentiful; a ready market for tobacco existed; even the yeoman farmer could rise rapidly if he could make the transition to staple production; and above all there was a quick recognition of accomplishment, by a standard which was not available in England but which was the only one available in Virginia: success in creating a plantation.

The decade of the 1660's inaugurated by the restoration of the Stuart monarchy, marked something of a turning point in the fortunes of the colony not unrelated to the movement there and in Maryland to fix irrevocably upon the Negro a lifetime of slavery. It was during this decade that certain factors bearing upon the colony's economic future were precipitated. One such factor was a serious drop in tobacco prices, brought on not only by overproduction but also by the Navigation Acts of 1660 and 1661, and the market was not to be fully restored for another twenty years. This meant, with rising costs and a disappearing margin of profit, that commercial production on a small-scale basis was placed under serious disabilities. Another factor was the rise in the slave population. Whereas there had been only about 300 in 1650, by 1670 there were, according to Governor Berkeley, 2,000 slaves in a servant population of 8,000. This was already 25 per cent of the servants, and the figure was

even more significant for the future, since the total white servant population in any given period could never be counted on to exceed their average annual immigration multiplied by five or six (the usual term in years of their indenture), while the increase of slaves over the same period would be cumulative. Such a development would by now be quite enough to stimulate the leaders of the colony—virtually all planters —to clarify in law once and for all the status of lifetime Negro servitude. The formation in 1662 of a Royal Company of Adventurers for the importation of Negroes symbolized the crown's expectation that a labor force of slaves would be the coming thing in the colonies.

It was thus in a period of relatively hard times that it became clear, if the colony of Virginia were to prosper, that capitalism would be the dynamic force in its economic life. "Success" could no longer be visualized as a rise from small beginnings, as it once could, but must now be conceived as a matter of substantial initial investments in land, equipment, and labor, plus the ability to undertake large annual commitments on credit. With the fall in tobacco prices, and with the tiny margin of profit that remained, the yeoman farmer found it difficult enough to eke out a bare living, let alone think of competing with the large planter or of purchasing slaves' or servants' indentures. Success was still possible, but now its terms were clearer, and those who achieved it would be fewer in numbers. The man who managed it would be the man with the large holdings—the man who could command a substantial force of laborers, white or black—who could afford a sizable yearly investment in the handling of his crop: in short, the capitalist planter.

The period beginning in the 1680's and ending about 1710 marked still a new phase. It saw, now under conditions of comparative prosperity, the full emergence of the plantation as the basic unit of capitalist agriculture. By about 1680 the market for Virginia and Maryland tobacco had been restored, though it is important to note that this was accompanied by no great rise in prices. It was rather a matter of having recaptured the European market by flooding it with cheap tobacco and underselling competitors. Returning prosperity, therefore, meant something far more concrete to the man with resources, who could produce tobacco in large enough amounts to make a slim profit margin worthwhile, than to the one whose productivity was limited by the acreage which he and his family could work. These years also witnessed the initial exploitation of the Carolinas, a process which moved much more directly toward large agricultural units than had been the case in Virginia. The acceleration of this development toward clarifying the terms of commercial production—large plantations and substantial investments—had a direct connection with the widening of the market for slaves during this same period. Hand in hand with large holdings went slaves—an assumption which was now being taken more or less for granted. "A rational man," wrote a South Carolina colonist in 1682, "will certainly inquire, 'when I have Land, what shall I doe with it? What commoditys shall I be able to produce, that will yield me money in other countrys, that I may be inabled to buy Negro-slaves, (without which a planter can never doe any great matter)?' " The point had clearly passed when white servants could realistically, on any long-term appraisal, be considered preferable to Negro slaves. Such appraisals were now being made in terms of capitalized earning power, a concept appropriate to large operations rather than small, to long-term rather than short-term planning.

It was, of course, only the man of means who could afford to think in this way. But then he is the one who most concerns us—the man responsible for Negro slavery. Determined in the sixties and seventies to make money despite hard times and low prices, and willing to undertake the investments which that required, he could now in the eighties reap the fruits of his foresight. His slaves were more valuable than ever—a monument to his patience and planning. What had made them so? For one thing he, unlike the yeoman farmer, had a large establishment for training them and was not pressed by the need, as he would have been with white servants on limited indenture, to exploit their *immediate* labor. The labor was his permanently. And for another thing, the system was by now just old enough to make clear for the first time the full meaning of a second generation of native-born American Negroes. These were the dividends: slaves born to the work and using Engish as their native tongue. By the 1690's the demand for slaves in the British colonies had become so great, and the Royal African Company so inefficient in supplying them, that in 1698 Parliament revoked the company's monopoly on the African coast and threw open the traffic to independent merchants and traders. The stream of incoming slaves, already of some consequence, now became enormous, and at the same time the annual flow of white servants to Virginia and the Carolinas dropped sharply. By 1710 it had become virtually negligible.

What meaning might all this have had for the legal status of the Negro? The connection was intimate and direct; with the full development of the plantation there was nothing, so far as his interests were concerned, to prevent unmitigated capitalism from becoming unmitigated slavery. The planter was now engaged in capitalistic agriculture with a labor force entirely under his control. The personal relationship between master and slave—in any case less likely to exist on large agricultural units than on smaller ones—now became far less important than the economic necessities which had forced the slave into this "unnatural" organization in the first place. For the plantation to operate efficiently and profitably, and with a force of laborers not all of whom may have been fully broken to plantation discipline, the necessity of training them to work long hours and to give unquestioning obedience to their masters and overseers superseded every other consideration. The master must have absolute power over the slave's body, and the law was developing in such a way as to give it to him at every crucial point.

Physical discipline was made virtually unlimited and the slave's chattel status unalterably fixed. It was in such a setting that those rights of personality traditionally regarded between men as private and inherent, quite apart from the matter of lifetime servitude, were left virtually without defense. The integrity of the family was ignored, and slave marriage was deprived of any legal or moral standing. The condition of a bondsman's soul—a matter of much concern to church and civil authority in the Spanish colonies—was here very quickly dropped from consideration. A series of laws enacted between 1667 and 1671 had systematically removed any lingering doubts whether conversion to Christianity should make a difference in status: henceforth it made none. The balance, therefore, involved on the one side the constant pressure of costs, prices, and the problems of management, and on the other the personal interests of the slave. Here, there were no counterweights: those interests were unsupported by any social pressures from the outside; they were cherished by no customary feudal immunities; they were no concern of the government (the king's main interest was in tobacco revenue); they could not be sustained by the church, for the church had little enough power and influence among its own white constituencies, to say nothing of the suspicion its ministers aroused at every proposal to enlarge the church's work among the blacks. The local planter class controlled all those public concerns which most affected the daily life of the colony, and it was thus only in matters of the broadest and most general policy that this planter domination was in any way touched by bureaucratic decisions made in London. The emergent institution of slavery was in effect unchallenged by any other institutions.

The result was that the slave, utterly powerless, would at every critical point see his interests further depressed. At those very points the drive of the law —unembarrassed by the perplexities of competing interests—was to clarify beyond all question, to rationalize, to simplify, and to make more logical and symmetrical the slave's status in society. So little impeded was this pressure to define and clarify that all the major categories in law which bore upon such status were very early established with great thoroughness and completeness. The unthinking aggressions upon the slave's personality which such a situation made possible becomes apparent upon an examination, in greater detail, of these legal categories.

SLAVERY IN CAPITALIST AND NON-CAPITALIST CULTURES

The four major legal categories which defined the status of the American slave may be roughly classified as "term of servitude," "marriage and the family," "police and disciplinary powers over the slave" and "property and other civil rights." The first of these, from which somehow all the others flowed, had in effect been established during the latter half of the seventeenth century; a slave was a slave for the duration of his life, and slavery was a status which he transmitted by inheritance to his children and his children's children.

It would be fairest, for several reasons, to view the remaining three categories in terms of the jurisprudence of the nineteenth century. By that time the most savage aspects of slavery from the standpoint of Southern practice (and thus, to a certain extent, of law) had become greatly softened. We may accordingly see it in its most humane light and at the same time note the clarity with which its basic outlines remained fixed and embodied in law, much as they had been laid down before the middle of the eighteenth century.

That most ancient and intimate of institutional arrangements, marriage and the family, had long since been destroyed by the law, and the law never showed any inclination to rehabilitate it. Here was the area in which considerations of humanity might be expected most widely to prevail, and, indeed, there is every reason to suppose that on an informal daily basis they did: the contempt in which respectable society held the slave trader, who separated mother from child and husband from wife, is proverbial in Southern lore. On the face of things, it ought to have been simple enough to translate this strong social sentiment into the appropriate legal enactments, which might systematically have guaranteed the inviolability of the family and the sanctity of the marriage bond, such as governed Christian polity everywhere. Yet the very nature of the plantation economy and the way in which the basic arrangements of Southern life radiated from it, made it inconceivable that the law should tolerate any ambiguity, should the painful clash between humanity and property interest ever occur. Any restrictions on the separate sale of slaves would have been reflected immediately in the market; their price would have dropped considerably. Thus the law could permit no aspect of the slave's conjugal state to have an independent legal existence outside the power of the man who owned him: ...

It would thus go without saying that the offspring of such "contubernial relationships," as they were called, had next to no guaranties against indiscriminate separation from their parents. Of additional interest is the fact that children derived their condition from that of their mother. This was not unique to American slavery, but it should be noted that especially in a system conceived and evolved exclusively on grounds of property there could be little doubt about how such a question would be resolved. Had status been defined according to the father's condition—as was briefly the case in seventeenth-century Maryland, following the ancient common law—there would instantly have arisen the irksome question of what to do with the numerous mulatto children born every year of white planter-fathers and slave mothers. It would have meant the creation of a free mulatto class, automatically relieving the master of so many slaves on the one hand, while burdening him on the other with that many colored children whom he could not own. Such equivocal relationships were never permitted to vex the law. That "the father of a slave is unknown to our law" was the universal understanding of Southern jurists. It was thus that a father, among slaves, was legally "unknown," a husband without the rights of his bed, the state of marriage defined as "only that concubinage . . . with which alone, perhaps, their condition is compatible," and motherhood clothed in the scant dignity of the breeding function.

Regarding matters of police and discipline, it is hardly necessary to view the typical slave's lot in the nineteenth century as one of stripes and torture. . . . Yet here again what impresses us is not the laxity with which much of the daily discipline was undoubtedly handled, but rather the completeness with which such questions, even extending to life and limb, were in fact under the master's dominion. "On our estates," wrote the Southern publicist J. D. B. DeBow in 1853, "we dispense with the whole machinery of public police and public courts of justice. Thus we try, decide, and execute the sentences in thousands of cases, which in other countries would go into the courts." The law deplored "cruel and unusual punishment." But wherever protection was on the one hand theoretically extended, it was practically canceled on the other by the universal prohibition in Southern law against permitting slaves to testify in court, except against each other, and in any case the courts generally accepted the principle that the line between correction and cruelty was impossible to determine. . . . In general, the court's primary care— not only in the killing of slaves by persons other than the master but also in cases where the slave himself had committed murder and was executed by the state—was for the pecuniary interest of the owner. Numerous enactments provided for compensation in either event. It was precisely this pecuniary interest which was at the very heart of legal logic on all such questions. Just as it was presumed to operate against "cruel and unusual punishment," so it became virtually a *non sequitur* that a man should kill his own slave. The principle had been enunciated very early: "It cannot be presumed that prepensed malice (which alone makes murder felony) should induce any man to destroy his own estate."

The rights of property, and all other civil and legal "rights," were everywhere denied the slave with a clarity that left no doubt of his utter dependency upon his master. . . . He could neither give nor receive gifts; he could make no will, nor could he, by will, inherit anything. He could not hire himself out or make contracts for any purpose—even including, as we have seen, that of matrimony— and thus neither his word nor his bond had any standing in law. He could buy or sell nothing at all, except as his master's agent, could keep no cattle, horses, hogs, or sheep and, in Mississippi at least, could raise no cotton. Even masters who permitted such transactions, except under express arrangement, were uniformly liable to fines. It was obvious, then, that the case of a slave who should presume to buy his own freedom—he being unable to possess money—would involve a legal absurdity. "Slaves have no legal rights in things, real or personal; but whatever they may acquire, belongs, in point of law, to their masters."

Such proscriptions were extended not only over all civil rights but even to the civic privileges of education and worship. Every Southern state except Maryland and Kentucky had stringent laws forbidding anyone to teach slaves reading and writing, and in some states the penalties applied to the educating of free Negroes and mulattoes as well. It was thought that "teaching slaves to read and write tends to dissatisfaction in their minds, and to produce insurrection and rebellion"; in North Carolina it was a crime to distribute among them any pamphlet or book, not excluding the Bible. The same apprehensions applied to instruction in religion. Southern society was not disposed to withhold the consolations of divine worship from its slaves, but the conditions would have to be laid down not by the church as an institution, not even by the planters as laity, but by planters simply as masters.

*   *   *

It is true that among the most attractive features of the plantation legend, dear to every Southerner with a sense of his past, were the paternal affection of the good master for his blacks and the warm sentiments entertained in Southern society at large for the faithful slave. The other side of the coin, then, might appear as something of a paradox: the most implacable race-consciousness yet observed in virtually any society. It was evolved in the Southern mind, one might say, as a simple syllogism, the precision of whose terms paralleled the precision of the system itself. All slaves are black; slaves are degraded and contemptible; therefore all blacks are degraded and contemptible and should be kept in a state of slavery. How had the simple syllogism come into being? That very strength and bulwark of American society, capitalism, unimpeded by prior arrangements and institutions, had stamped the status of slave upon the black with a clarity which elsewhere could never have been so profound, and had further defined the institution of slavery with such nicety that the slave *was,* in fact, degraded. That the black, as a species, was thus contemptible seemed to follow by observation. This assumption took on a life of its own in the attitudes of the people, and the very thought of such a creature existing outside the pale of their so aptly devised system filled the most reasonable of Southerners with fear and loathing. Quite apart from the demands of the system itself, this may account for many of the subsidiary social taboos— the increasing severity of the laws against manumission, the horror of miscegenation, the depressed condition of the free Negro and his peculiar place in Southern society: all signs of how difficult it was to conceive a non-slave colored class. Nothing in their experience had prepared them for it; such a class was unnatural, logically awry, a blemish on the body politic, an anomaly for which there was no intellectual category. . . .

The basic fact was, of course, that the slave himself was property. He and his fellow bondsmen had long since become "chattels personal . . . to all intents, constructions and purposes whatsoever."

In the slave system of the United States—so finely circumscribed and so cleanly self-contained—virtually all avenues of recourse for the slave, all lines of communication to society at large, originated and ended with the master. The system was unique, *sui generis*. The closest parallel to it at that time was to be found in the Latin-American colonies of Spain and Portugal. But the differences between the two systems are so much more striking than the similarities that we may with profit use them not as parallels but as contrasts. In the Spanish and Portuguese colonies, we are immediately impressed by the comparative lack of precision and logic governing the institution of slavery there; we find an exasperating dimness of line between the slave and free portions of society, a multiplicity of points of contact between the two, a confusing promiscuity of color, such as would never have been thinkable in our own country. But before attempting to establish legal and customary classifications on the slave's condition in these places, in some manner corresponding to those we used for the United States, something should be said about the social and institutional setting in which slavery, in Spain and Portugal themselves, was both viewed and practiced.

*   *   *

Of all the national states of western Europe, Spain, though dynastically united to a substantial degree late in the fifteenth century (and having even absorbed Portugal in the sixteenth), remained, long into modern times, much the most "medieval." Its agriculture retained many of the subsistence features characteristic of manorial economy. Its social stability was guaranteed by that standing alliance of church and state upon which every feudal community rested; there, on a national scale, the Inquisition maintained at extravagant cost the dual secular-spiritual concept of society so characteristic of the Middle Ages and so repugnant to every modern idea. Moreover, having to deal with the Moslems on Spanish soil, the Spaniards had built crusades and the crusading temperament into their basic experience, where it actively remained long after the collapse of the other crusaders' states in Asia Minor. This fact had much to do with the failure to develop a banking and commercial class comparable to those existing elsewhere, for the chronic persecutions of the Moors and Jews deprived the kingdom of its most energetic and experienced businessmen. Banking services tended to be performed in very large part by foreigners, and Spanish wealth quickly found its way to places outside the realm. The monarchy's role in all such matters was conceived in a highly paternal and "illiberal" way, and laissez faire was just as unacceptable in economic life as was free-thinking in religion.

This royal paternalism was especially notable in colonial affairs and shows a striking contrast to the permissive policies which allowed so wide a latitude of local autonomy in the English colonies. The royal houses of Spain and Portugal had been the first in the race for overseas colonies—the crown and grandees having been rather more oriented to "glory" than to "success"—but they in time found themselves outstripped by the English and Dutch and saw the fruits of their glory dribble away to London, Antwerp, and other successful centers of banking. This lack of economic efficiency was not unconnected with the very administrative efficiency that permitted the Spanish crown to maintain such rigid control over its American dependencies. The degree of supervision exercised over colonial life by the Council of the Indies at Madrid does not seem to have been sufficiently appreciated. Add to this the power of the church, and the resulting setting may be seen as one hardly favorable to wide-scale enterprise. Even the establishment of great plantations in Cuba, Santo Domingo, Brazil, and elsewhere in the seventeenth and eighteenth centuries did not mean unmitigated capitalism, as would be the case under the free skies of Virginia, Maryland, and the Carolinas. The great difference lay in the fact that other institutional concerns were present besides those involved with production.

No such dramatic transvaluation of social norms as occurred in seventeenth-century England to accommodate the new standards of the bourgeoisie would ever take place in Spain. And nowhere could the chivalric concept of the *hidalgo,* the man who did no work with his hands and to whom business was contemptible, persist so tenaciously as in Spain and the Spanish colonies. There, on the other hand, the concept of private property, peculiarly appropriate to the demands of an entrepreneurial class, would not develop with nearly the elaborateness that characterized it elsewhere. In at least one area—the master-slave relationship—this fact had very important consequences. For all the cruelty and bigotry of this quasi-medieval society, the balance between property rights and human rights stood in a vastly different ratio—much to the advantage of human rights—from that seen in the American South.

In the colonies of Latin America we are thus able to think of the church, the civil authority, and the property concerns of the planter-adventurer as constituting distinct and not always harmonious interests in society. . . .

The Spaniards and Portuguese had the widespread reputation by the eighteenth century—whatever may have been the reasons—for being among all nations the best masters of slaves. The standards for such a judgment cannot, of course, be made too simple. Were slaves "physically maltreated" in those countries? They could, conceivably, have been treated worse than in our own nineteenth-century South without altering the comparison, for even in cruelty the relationship was between man and man. Was there "race prejudice"? No one could be more arrogantly proud of

his racial purity than the Spaniard of Castile, and theoretically there were rigid caste lines, but the finest Creole families, the clergy, the army, the professions, were hopelessly "defiled" by Negro blood; the taboos were that vague in practice. Was there squalor, filth, widespread depression of the masses? Much more so than with us—but there it was the class system and economic "underdevelopment," rather than the color barrier, that made the difference. In these countries the concept of "beyond the pale" applied primarily to beings outside the Christian fold rather than to those beyond the color line.

We are not, then, dealing with a society steeped, like our own, in traditions of political and economic democracy. We are concerned only with a special and peculiar kind of fluidity—that of their slave systems—and in this alone lay a world of difference. It was a fluidity that permitted a transition from slavery to freedom that was smooth, organic, and continuing. Manumitting slaves, carrying as it did such high social approval, was done often, and the spectacle of large numbers of freedmen was familiar to the social scene. Such opportunities as were open to any member of the depressed classes who had talent and diligence were open as well to the ex-slave and his descendants. Thus color itself was no grave disability against taking one's place in free society; indeed, Anglo-Saxon travelers in nineteenth-century Brazil were amazed at the thoroughgoing mixture of races there. "I have passed black ladies in silks and jewelry," wrote Thomas Ewbank in the 1850's, "with male slaves in livery behind them. . . . Several have white husbands. The first doctor of the city is a colored man; so is the President of the Province." Free Negroes had the same rights before the law as whites, and it was possible for the most energetic of their numbers to take immediate part in public and professional life. Among the Negroes and mulattoes of Brazil and the Spanish colonies—aside from the swarming numbers of skilled craftsmen—were soldiers, officers, musicians, poets, priests, and judges. "I am accustomed," said a delegate to the Cortes of Cádiz in 1811, "to seeing many engaged in all manner of careers."

All such rights and opportunities existed *before* the abolition of slavery; and thus we may note it as no paradox that emancipation, when it finally did take place, was brought about in all these Latin-American countries "without violence, without bloodshed, and without civil war."

The above set of contrasts, in addition to what it may tell us about slavery it-self, could also be of use for a more general problem, that of the conservative role of institutions in any social structure. The principle has been observed in one setting where two or more powerful interests were present to limit each other; it has been tested negatively in a setting where a single interest was free to develop without such limits. The latter case was productive of consequences which could hardly be called, in the classical sense of the term, "conservative."

Eugene D. Genovese

CAPITALIST AND PSEUDO-CAPITALIST FEATURES OF THE SLAVE ECONOMY

THE ORIGINS OF SLAVERY EXPANSIONISM

Professor Genovese, of Sir George Williams University (Montreal), in studying Southern agricultural development came to the conclusion that slavery exercised decisive influence over not only the economic life of the region, but over its social ideals as well. It was slavery that made the South a distinct nation-within-a-nation, in conflict with the capitalist mentality of the North and West. This theory, which has the neo-Beardian flavor of two civilizations locked in combat, was originally presented to counter the revisionist view that slavery was essentially plantation capitalism.

CAPITALIST AND PSEUDO-CAPITALIST FEATURES OF THE SLAVE ECONOMY

THE slave economy developed within, and was in a sense exploited by, the capitalist world market; consequently, slavery developed many ostensibly capitalist features, such as banking, commerce, and credit. These played a fundamentally different role in the South than in the North. . . .

We need to analyze a few of the more important capitalist and pseudo-capitalist features of Southern slavery and especially to review the barriers to industrialization in order to appreciate the peculiar qualities of this remarkable and anachronistic society.[7]

The defenders of the "planter-capitalism" thesis have noted the extensive

[7] This colonial dependence on the British and Northern markets did not end when slavery ended. Sharecropping and tenantry produced similar results. Since abolition occurred under Northern guns and under the program of a victorious, predatory outside bourgeoisie, instead of under internal bourgeois auspices, the colonial bondage of the economy was preserved, but the South's political independence was lost.

From *The Political Economy of Slavery*, by Eugene Genovese, pp. 19–23, 28–36, 243–251, 256–270. © Copyright 1961, 1963, 1965 by Eugene Genovese. Reprinted by permission of Pantheon Books, a Division of Random House, Inc.

commercial links between the plantation and the world market and the modest commercial bourgeoisie in the South
and have concluded that there is no
reason to predicate an antagonism between cotton producers and cotton merchants. However valid as a reply to the
naive arguments of the proponents
of the agrarianism-versus-industrialism
thesis, this criticism has unjustifiably
been twisted to suggest that the presence
of commercial activity proves the pre-
dominance of capitalism in the South.[8]
Many precapitalist economic systems
have had well-developed commercial relations, but if every commercial society
is to be considered capitalist, the word
loses all meaning. In general, commercial classes have supported the existing
system of production. . . .

We must concern ourselves primarily
with capitalism as a social system, not
merely with evidence of typically capitalistic economic practices. In the South
extensive and complicated commercial
relations with the world market permitted the growth of a small commercial
bourgeoisie. The resultant fortunes
flowed into slaveholding, which offered
prestige and economic and social security in a planter-dominated society. Independent merchants found their busi-
nesses dependent on the patronage of
the slaveholders. The merchants either
became planters themselves or assumed
a servile attitude toward the planters.
The commercial bourgeoisie, such as it
was, remained tied to the slaveholding
interest, had little desire or opportunity
to invest capital in industrial expansion,
and adopted the prevailing aristocratic
attitudes.

The Southern industrialists were in an
analogous position, although one that
was potentially subversive of the political power and ideological unity of the
planters. The preponderance of planters and slaves on the countryside re-
tarded the home market. The Southern
yeomanry, unlike the Western, lacked
the purchasing power to sustain rapid
industrial development.[10] The planters

spent much of their money abroad for
luxuries. The plantation market consisted primarily of the demand for cheap
slave clothing and cheap agricultural
implements for use or misuse by the
slaves. Southern industrialism needed
a sweeping agrarian revolution to provide it with cheap labor and a substantial
rural market, but the Southern industrialists depended on the existing, limited, plantation market. . . .

If for a moment we accept the desig-
nation of the planters as capitalists and
the slave system as a form of capitalism,
we are then confronted by a capitalist
society that impeded the development of
every normal feature of capitalism. The
planters were not mere capitalists; they
were precapitalist, quasi-aristocratic
landowners who had to adjust their
economy and ways of thinking to a capitalist world market. Their society, in its
spirit and fundamental direction, represented the antithesis of capitalism,
however many compromises it had to
make. The fact of slave ownership is
central to our problem. This seemingly
formal question of whether the owners
of the means of production command
labor or purchase the labor power of
free workers contains in itself the content of Southern life. The essential features of Southern particularity, as well
as of Southern backwardness, can be
traced to the relationship of master to
slave. . . .

The banking system of the South
serves as an excellent illustration of an
ostensibly capitalist institution that
worked to augment the power of the
planters and retard the development of
the bourgeoisie. Southern banks func-
tioned much as did those which the
British introduced into Latin America,
India, and Egypt during the nineteenth
century. Although the British banks fos-
tered dependence on British capital, they

---

[8] Govan, *JSH*, XXI (Nov. 1955), 448.
[10] An attempt was made by Frank L. Owsley and

his students to prove that the Southern yeomanry was strong and prosperous. For a summary treatment see *Plain Folk of the Old South*
(Baton Rouge, La., 1949). This view was con-
vincingly refuted by Fabian Linden, "Economic
Democracy in the Slave South: An Appraisal of
Some Recent Views," *JNH*, XXXI (April 1946),
140–89.

did not directly and willingly generate internal capitalist development. They were not sources of industrial capital but "large-scale clearing houses of mercantile finance vying in their interest charges with the local usurers."[11] . . .

The slave states paid considerable attention to the development of a conservative, stable banking system, which could guarantee the movement of staple crops and the extension of credit to the planters. Southern banks were primarily designed to lend the planters money for outlays that were economically feasible and socially acceptable in a slave society: the movement of crops, the purchase of land and slaves, and little else.

Whenever Southerners pursued easy-credit policies, the damage done outweighed the advantages of increased production. This imbalance probably did not occur in the West, for easy credit made possible agricultural and industrial expansion of a diverse nature and, despite acute crises, established a firm basis for long-range prosperity. Easy credit in the South led to expansion of cotton production with concomitant over-production and low prices; simultaneously, it increased the price of slaves.

Planters wanted their banks only to facilitate cotton shipments and maintain sound money. They purchased large quantities of foodstuffs from the West and, since they shipped little in return, had to pay in bank notes. For five years following the bank failures of 1837 the bank notes of New Orleans moved at a discount of from 10 to 25 per cent. This disaster could not be allowed to recur. Sound money and sound banking became the cries of the slaveholders as a class.

Southern banking tied the planters to the banks, but more important, tied the bankers to the plantations. The banks often found it necessary to add prominent planters to their boards of directors and were closely supervised by the planter-dominated state legislatures. In this relationship the bankers could not

[11] Paul A. Baran, *The Political Economy of Growth* (New York, 1957), p. 194.

emerge as a middle-class counterweight to the planters but could merely serve as their auxiliaries.

The bankers of the free states also allied themselves closely with the dominant producers, but society and economy took on a bourgeois quality provided by the rising industrialists, the urban middle classes, and the farmers who increasingly depended on urban markets. The expansion of credit, which in the West financed manufacturing, mining, transportation, agricultural diversification, and the numerous branches of a capitalist economy, in the South bolstered the economic position of the planters, inhibited the rise of alternative industries, and guaranteed the extension and consolidation of the plantation system.

THE IDEOLOGY OF THE MASTER CLASS

The planters commanded Southern politics and set the tone of social life. Theirs was an aristocratic, antibourgeois spirit with values and mores emphasizing family and status, a strong code of honor, and aspirations to luxury, ease, and accomplishment. In the planters' community, paternalism provided the standard of human relationships, and politics and statecraft were the duties and responsibilities of gentlemen. The gentleman lived for politics, not, like the bourgeois politician, off politics.

The planter typically recoiled at the notions that profit should be the goal of life; that the approach to production and exchange should be internally rational and uncomplicated by social values; that thrift and hard work should be the great virtues; and that the test of the wholesomeness of a community should be the vigor with which its citizens expand the economy. The planter was no less acquisitive than the bourgeois, but an acquisitive spirit is compatible with values antithetical to capitalism. The aristocratic spirit of the planters absorbed acquisitiveness and directed it into channels that were socially desirable to a slave society: the accumulation of slaves and land and the achievement of military and political honors. Whereas in the North people followed the lure of business and money for their own sake, in the South specific forms of property carried the badges of honor, prestige, and power. Even the rough parvenu planters of the Southwestern frontier—the "Southern Yankees"—strove to accumulate wealth in the modes acceptable to plantation society. Only in their crudeness and naked avarice did they differ from the Virginia gentlemen. They were a generation removed from the refinement that follows accumulation.

Slavery established the basis of the planter's position and power. It measured his affluence, marked his status, and supplied leisure for social graces and aristocratic duties. The older bourgeoisie of New England in its own way struck an aristocratic pose, but its wealth was rooted in commercial and industrial enterprises that were being pushed into the background by the newer heavy industries arising in the West, where upstarts took advantage of the more lucrative ventures like the iron industry. In the South few such opportunities were opening. The parvenu differed from the established planter only in being cruder and perhaps sharper in his business dealings. The road to power lay through the plantation. The older aristocracy kept its leadership or made room for men following the same road. An aristocratic stance was no mere compensation for a decline in power; it was the soul and content of a rising power. . . .

The prevailing attitude of the aristocratic South toward itself and its Northern rival was ably summed up by William Henry Holcombe of Natchez: "The Northerner loves to make money, the Southerner to spend it."[21]

At their best, Southern ideals constituted a rejection of the crass, vulgar, inhumane elements of capitalist society. The slaveholders simply could not accept the idea that the cash nexus offered a permissible basis for human relations. Even the vulgar parvenu of the Southwest embraced the plantation myth and refused to make a virtue of necessity by glorifying the competitive side of slavery

as civilization's highest achievement. The slaveholders generally, and the planters in particular, did identify their own ideals with the essence of civilization and, given their sense of honor, were prepared to defend them at any cost.

This civilization and its ideals were antinational in a double sense. The plantation offered virtually the only market for the small nonstaple-producing farmers and provided the center of necessary services for the small cotton growers. Thus, the paternalism of the planters toward their slaves was reinforced by the semipaternal relationship between the planters and their neighbors. The planters, in truth, grew into the closest thing to feudal lords imaginable in a nineteenth-century bourgeois republic. The planters' protestations of love for the Union were not so much a desire to use the Union to protect slavery as a strong commitment to localism as the highest form of liberty. They genuinely loved the Union so long as it alone among the great states of the world recognized that localism had a wide variety of rights. The Southerners' source of pride was not the Union, nor the nonexistent Southern nation; it was the plantation, which they raised to a political principle.

THE INNER REALITY OF SLAVEHOLDING

The Southern slaveholder had "extraordinary force." In the eyes of an admirer his independence was "not as at the North, the effect of a conflict with the too stern pressure of society, but the legitimate outgrowth of a sturdy love of liberty."[22] This independence, so distinctive in the slaveholders' psychology, divided them politically from agrarian Westerners as well as from urban Easterners. Commonly, both friendly and hostile contemporaries agreed that the Southerner appeared rash, unstable, often irrational, and that he turned away from bourgeois habits toward an aristocratic pose. . . .

The slaveholder, as distinct from the farmer, had a private source of character making and mythmaking—his slave.

[21] Diary dated Aug. 25, 1855, but clearly written later. Ms. in the University of North Carolina.

[22] William M. Sanford (?), *Southern Dial*, I (Nov. 1857), 9.

Most obviously, he had the habit of command, but there was more than despotic authority in this master-slave relationship. The slave stood interposed between his master and the object his master desired (that which was produced); thus, the master related to the object only mediately, through the slave. The slaveholder commanded the products of another's labor, but by the same process was forced into dependence upon this other.[23]

Thoughtful Southerners such as Ruffin, Fitzhugh, and Hammond understood this dependence and saw it as arising from the general relationship of labor to capital, rather than from the specific relationship of master to slave. They did not grasp that the capitalist's dependence upon his laborers remains obscured by the process of exchange in the capitalist market. Although all commodities are products of social relationships and contain human labor, they face each other in the market not as the embodiment of human qualities but as things with a seemingly independent existence. Similarly, the laborer sells his labor-power in the way in which the capitalist sells his goods—by bringing it to market, where it is subject to the fluctuations of supply and demand. A "commodity fetishism" clouds the social relationship of labor to capital, and the worker and capitalist appear as mere observers of a process over which they have little control.[24] Southerners correctly viewed the relationship as a general one of labor to capital but failed to realize that the capitalist's dependence on his laborers is hidden, whereas that of master on slave is naked. . . .

This simultaneous dependence and independence contributed to that peculiar combination of the admirable and the frightening in the slaveholder's nature: his strength, graciousness, and gentility; his impulsiveness, violence, and unsteadiness. The sense of independence and the habit of command developed his poise, grace, and dignity, but the less

[23] *Cf.* G. W. F. Hegel, *The Phenomenology of Mind* (2 vols.; London, 1910), I, 183 ff.
[24] *Cf* Karl Marx, *Capital* (3 vols.; New York, 1947), I, 41–55.

obvious sense of dependence on a despised other made him violently intolerant of anyone and anything threatening to expose the full nature of his relationship to his slave. Thus, he had a far deeper conservatism than that usually attributed to agrarians. His independence stood out as his most prized possession, but the instability of its base produced personal rashness and directed that rashness against any alteration in the status quo. Any attempt, no matter how well meaning, indirect, or harmless, to question the slave system appeared not only as an attack on his material interests but as an attack on his self-esteem at its most vulnerable point. To question either the morality or the practicality of slavery meant to expose the root of the slaveholder's dependence in independence.

THE GENERAL CRISIS
OF THE SLAVE SOUTH

The South's slave civilization could not forever coexist with an increasingly hostile, powerful, and aggressive Northern capitalism. On the one hand, the special economic conditions arising from the dependence on slave labor bound the South, in a colonial manner, to the world market. The concentration of landholding and slaveholding prevented the rise of a prosperous yeomanry and of urban centers. The inability to build urban centers restricted the market for agricultural produce, weakened the rural producers, and dimmed hopes for agricultural diversification. On the other hand, the same concentration of wealth, the isolated, rural nature of the plantation system, the special psychology engendered by slave ownership, and the political opportunity presented by the separation from England, converged to give the South considerable political and social independence. This independence was primarily the contribution of the slaveholding class, and especially of the planters. Slavery, while it bound the South economically, granted it the privilege of developing an aristocratic tradition, a disciplined and cohesive ruling class, and a mythology of its own.

Aristocratic tradition and ideology intensified the South's attachment to economic backwardness. Paternalism and the habit of command made the slaveholders tough stock, determined to defend their Southern heritage. The more economically debilitating their way of life, the more they clung to it. It was this side of things—the political hegemony and aristocratic ideology of the ruling class—rather than economic factors that prevented the South from relinquishing slavery voluntarily.

As the free states stepped up their industrialization and as the westward movement assumed its remarkable momentum, the South's economic and political allies in the North were steadily isolated. Years of abolitionist and free-soil agitation bore fruit as the South's opposition to homesteads, tariffs, and internal improvements clashed more and more dangerously with the North's economic needs. To protect their institutions and to try to lessen their economic bondage, the slaveholders slid into violent collision with Northern interests and sentiments. The economic deficiencies of slavery threatened to undermine the planters' wealth and power. Such relief measures as cheap labor and more land for slave states (reopening the slave trade and territorial expansion) conflicted with Northern material needs, aspirations, and morality.[26] The planters

faced a steady deterioration of their political and social power. Even if the relative prosperity of the 1850s had continued indefinitely, the slave states would have been at the mercy of the free, which steadily forged ahead in population growth, capital accumulation, and economic development. Any economic slump threatened to bring with it an internal political disaster, for the slaveholders could not rely on their middle and lower classes to remain permanently loyal.[27]

When we understand that the slave South developed neither a strange form of capitalism nor an undefinable agrarianism but a special civilization built on the relationship of master to slave, we expose the root of its conflict with the North. The internal contradictions in the South and the external conflict with the North placed the slaveholders hopelessly on the defensive with little to look forward to except slow strangulation. Their only hope lay in a bold stroke to complete their political independence and to use it to provide an expansionist solution for their economic and social problems. The ideology and psychology of the proud slaveholding class made surrender or resignation to gradual defeat unthinkable, for its fate, in its own eyes at least, was the fate of everything worthwhile in Western civilization.

---

[26] These measures met opposition from powerful sections of the slaveholding class for reasons that cannot be discussed here. The independence of the South would only have brought the latent intraclass antagonisms to the surface.

[27] The loyalty of these classes was real but unstable. For our present purposes let us merely note that Lincoln's election and federal patronage would, if Southern fears were justified, have led to the formation of an antiplanter party in the South.

THE ORIGINS OF SLAVERY EXPANSIONISM

Once upon a time in the happy and innocent days of the nineteenth century, men believed that Negro slavery had raised an expansionist slaveocracy to power in the American South. Today we know better. The revisionists have denied that slavery was expansionist and have virtually driven their opponents from the field. Their arguments, as distinct from their faith in the possibilities of resolving antagonisms peacefully

rest on two formidable essays. In 1926, Avery O. Craven published his *Soil Exhaustion as a Factor in the Agricultural History of Maryland and Virginia,* which sought to prove that the slave economy could reform itself, and three years later Charles William Ramsdell published his famous article on "The Natural Limits of Slavery Expansion,"[1] which consti-

---

[1] *AHR,* XVI (Sept. 1929), 151–71.

tuted a frontal attack on the "irrepressible conflict" school.

I propose to restate the traditional view, but in such a way as to avoid the simplistic and mechanistic notions of Cairnes and his followers and to account for the data that has emerged from the conscientious and often splendid researches of the revisionist historians. Specifically, I propose to show that economics, politics, social life, ideology, and psychology converged to thrust the system outward and that beneath each factor lay the exigencies of the slaveholding class. Each dictated expansion if the men who made up the ruling class of the South were to continue to rule.

ROOTS AND TAPROOT

Antebellum Southern economic history reinforces rather than overturns the nineteenth-century notion of an expansionist slaveocracy. That notion undoubtedly suffered from grave defects and considerable crudeness, for it insisted on the lack of versatility of slave labor and the steady deterioration of the soil without appreciating the partially effective attempts to reform the slave economy. Yet the revisionist work of the Craven school, which has contributed so much toward an understanding of the economic complexities, has not added up to a successful refutation.

We may recapitulate briefly the main points of the preceding studies, which lead to the economic root of slavery expansionism. At the beginning we encounter the low productivity of slave labor, defined not according to some absolute or purely economic standard, but according to the political exigencies of the slaveholders. The slaves worked well enough in the cotton and sugar fields, when organized in gangs, but the old criticism of labor given grudgingly retains its force.

Slave labor lacked that degree and kind of versatility which would have permitted general agricultural diversification. Slaves could and did work in a variety of pursuits, including industrial, but under circumstances not easily created within the economy as a whole. Division of labor on the plantations and in society proceeded slowly and under great handicaps. The level of technology, especially on the plantations, was kept low by the quality and size of the labor force. Mules and oxen, for example, replaced faster horses principally because they could more easily withstand rough and perhaps vengeful handling. Negro laborers had been disciplined to sustained agricultural labor before being brought to the Americas. Their low productivity arose from the human and technological conditions under which they worked, and these arose from the slave system.

An analysis of Southern livestock and the attempts to improve it reveals the complex and debilitating interrelationships within the slave economy. The South had more than enough animals to feed its population but had to import meat. A shortage of liquid capital made acquisition of better breeds difficult, and the poor treatment of the animals by the slaves made maintenance of any reasonable standards close to impossible. As a further complication, the lack of urban markets inhibited attention to livestock by depriving planters of outlets for potential surpluses. The South boasted an enormous number of animals but suffered from their wretched quality.

Slavery provided a sufficient although not a necessary cause of soil exhaustion. It dictated one-crop production beyond the limits of commercial advantage and in opposition to the political safety of the slaveholders. Planters could not easily rotate crops under the existing credit structure, with a difficult labor force, and without those markets which could only accompany industrial and urban advance. The sheer size of the plantations discouraged fertilization. Barnyard manure was scarce, commercial fertilizers too expensive, and the care necessary for advantageous application unavailable. The shortage of good implements complicated the operation, for manures are easily wasted when not applied properly.

Craven insists that the existence of a moving frontier, north and south, brought about the same result, but as we have seen, the special force of slavery cannot so easily be brushed aside. The North confronted the devastating effects of soil exhaustion and built a diversified economy in the older areas as the frontier pushed westward. The South, faced with the debilitating effects of slavery long after the frontier had passed, had to struggle against hopeless odds.

These direct effects of slavery received enormous reinforcement from such indirect effects as the shortage of capital and entrepreneurship and the weakness of the market. Capital investments in slaves and a notable tendency toward aristocratic consumption had their economic advantages but inhibited the rise of new industries. The Southern market consisted primarily of the plantations and could not support more than a limited industrial advance. The restricted purchasing power of the rural whites, of the urban lower classes, and indirectly of the slaves hemmed in Southern manufacturers and put them at a severe competitive disadvantage relative to Northerners, who had had a head start and who had much wider markets in the free states to sustain production on an increasing scale. The barriers to industrialization also blocked urbanization and thereby undermined the market for foodstuffs. . . .

The South made one form of agricultural adjustment while slavery remained. The great agricultural revival in the Upper South overcame the most serious effects of slavery by reducing the size of slaveholdings, converting surplus slaves into cash, and investing the funds in the supervision, fertilization, and reconversion of smaller estates. This process threatened the economic and ideological solidity of the slaveholders' regime and had other drawbacks, but most important, it broke on an immanent contradiction. The sale of surplus slaves depended on markets further south, which necessarily depended on virgin lands on which to apply the old, wasteful methods of farming. Reform in one region implied exhaustive agriculture in another. Thus, the process of agricultural reform had narrow limits in a closed slave system and had to be re-versed when it pressed against them. No solution emerged from within the system, but one beckoned from without. The steady acquisition of new land could alone guarantee the maintenance of that interregional slave trade which held the system together. . . .

The economic process propelling the slave South along expansionist paths had its political and social parallels, the most obvious being the need to re-establish parity in the Senate or at least to guarantee enough voting strength in Washington to protect Southern interests. In an immediate political sense the demand for more slave-state Congressmen was among the important roots of expansionism, but in a deeper sense it was merely a symptom of something more fundamental. Had the South not had a distinct social system to preserve and a distinct and powerful ruling class at its helm, a decline of its political and economic power would have caused no greater alarm than it did in New England.

A second political root was the need to protect slavery where it was profitable by establishing buffer areas where it might not be. Just as the British had to spend money to secure ascendancy in Tibet so that they could make money in India, the South had to establish political control over areas with dubious potentialities as slave states in order to protect existing slave states. The success of the Texas cause removed the fear of Mexican tampering with slaves in Louisiana, much as annexation removed potential British-inspired tampering. "Texas must be a slave country," wrote Stephen F. Austin to his sister. "The interest of Louisiana requires that it should be; a population of fanatical abolitionists in Texas would have a very pernicious and dangerous influence on the overgrown population of the state."[2] . . .

The warning of the Louisville *Daily Courier* in 1860 that Kentucky could afford to remain in the Union but that the Lower South could not touched the cen-

[2] Quoted in Herbert Aptheker, *American Negro Slave Revolts* (New York, 1963), pp. 32–33.

tral issue. Suppose, it asked, Kentucky sold its slaves south. "And then what? Antislavery will not be content to rest. . . . The war will be transferred to the Cotton States."[7]

The need to push forward in order to ward off concentrations of hostile power arose from the anachronistic nature of the slave regime. By 1850, if not much earlier, world opinion could no longer tolerate chattel slavery, and British opposition in particular was both formidable and implacable. The transformation of the Caribbean into a slaveholders' lake and an alliance or understanding with Brazil held out the only hope of preventing a dangerous and tightening containment.

Slaveholders also sought additional territory to reduce the danger of internal convulsion. Lieutenant Matthew F. Maury, who helped bring about the American exploration of the Amazon Valley in the 1850s, discussed the eventual absorption of much of Latin America by the United States:

I cannot be blind to what I see going on here. It is becoming a matter of *faith*—I use a strong word—yes a matter of faith among leading Southern men, that the time is coming, nay that it is rapidly approaching when in order to prevent this war of the races and all its horrors, they will in self-defense be compelled to conquer parts of Mexico and Central America, and make slave territory of that—and that is now free.[8]

Representative Thomas L. Clingman of North Carolina told the House that Northerners were "too intelligent to believe that humanity, either to the slave or the master, requires that they should be pent up within a territory which after a time will be insufficient for their subsistence, and where they must perish from want, or from collision that would occur between the races."[9] Southerners always kept the West Indian experience

in front of them when they discussed the racial proportions of the population.

Probably, steady infusions of new land were also needed to placate the nonslaveholders, but we know little about slaveholder-nonslaveholder relationships as yet and little can be said with certainty.

The psychological dimension of slavery expansionism has been the subject of various essays and has, for example, emerged from interpretations of Southern frustration and resultant aggression. We need not pursue esoteric lines of inquiry, especially with formulas so broad as to be able to encompass almost every society in any age, to appreciate that a psychological dimension did exist. As Southerners came to regard slavery as a positive good and as they came to value the civilization it made possible as the world's finest, they could hardly accept limits on its expansion. To agree to containment meant to agree that slavery constituted an evil, however necessary for the benefit of the savage Africans. That sense of mission so characteristic of the United States as a whole had its Southern manifestation in the mission of slavery. If slavery was making possible the finest society the world had ever known, the objections to its expansion were intolerable. The free-soil argument struck at the foundations of the slaveholder's pride and belief in himself.

*   *   *

When the more intelligent and informed Southerners demanded the West for slavery they often, perhaps most often, spoke of minerals, not cotton or even hemp. Slavery, from ancient times to modern, had proved itself splendidly adaptable to mining. Mining constituted one of the more important industries of the Negroes of preconquest Africa, and slave labor had a long history there. . . .

Closer in time and place to the South, Brazil afforded an impressive example of the successful use of slave labor in mining. In the middle of the eighteenth century diamond mining supplemented gold mining in Minas Gerais and accounted

[7] Dec. 20, 1860 in Dwight L. Dumond (ed.), *Southern Editorials on Secession* (New York, 1931), p. 360.
[8] Quoted in Aptheker, *Slave Revolts*, p. 34.
[9] Clingman, *Speeches*, p. 239.

for a massive transfer of masters and slaves from the northeastern sugar region.[12] Southern leaders knew a good deal about this experience. "The mines of Brazil," reported *De Bow's Review* in 1848, "are most prolific of iron, gold, and diamonds. . . . The operation is performed by negroes . . . 30,000 negroes have been so employed."[13] The eastern slave states had had experience with gold mining, and although the results were mixed, the potentialities of slave labor had been demonstrated.[14] Planters in the Southwestern states expressed interest in gold mines in Arkansas and hopefully looked further west.[15] "If mines of such temporary value should, as they may, be found in the territories, and slaves could be excluded from these," wrote A. F. Hopkins of Mobile in 1860, "it would present a case of monstrous injustice."[16]

During the Congressional debates of 1850, Representative Jacob Thompson of Mississippi, later to become Secretary of the Interior under Buchanan, expressed great concern over the fate of the public domain of California if she were to be hastily admitted to the Union and expressed special concern over the fate of the gold mines.[17] Ten years later, after a decade of similar warnings, pleas, hopes, and threats, S. D. Moore of Alabama wrote that the South was "excluded from California, not pretendedly even by 'isothermal lines,' or want of employment for slave labor, for in regard to climate and mining purposes the country was admirably adapted to

the institution of African slavery."[18] Had it not been for the antislavery agitation, Representative Clingman told the House in 1850, Southerners would have used slaves in the mines of California and transformed it into a slave state.[19] Albert Gallatin Brown, one of the most fiery and belligerent of the proslavery extremists, wrote his constituents that slave labor was admirably suited to mining and that California could and should be made into a slave state.[20] Even as a free state California demonstrated the usefulness of slave labor. In 1852 the state legislature passed a mischievous fugitive slave law that could be and was interpreted to allow slaveholders to bring slaves into the state to work in the mines and then send them home.[21]

Similarly, a Texan wrote in 1852 that a Mississippi and Pacific railroad would secure the New Mexico territory for the South by opening the mining districts to slave labor.[22] During the War for Southern Independence, Jefferson Davis received a communication from his Southwestern field commander that a successful drive to California would add "the most valuable agriculture and grazing lands, and the richest mineral region in the world."[23]

Southerners had long cast eyes toward Mexico and looked forward to additional annexations. "I want Cuba," roared Albert Gallatin Brown. "I want Tamaulipas, Potosí, and one or two other Mexican states; and I want them all for the same reason—for the planting or spreading of slavery."[24] Throughout the 1850s, *De Bow's Review* printed articles about Mexico and particularly about Mexican mines.

It is one thing to note that Southerners sought to expand slavery into Mexico's mining districts or that they la-

[12] João Pandía Calógeras, *A History of Brazil* (tr. Percy Alvin Martin; Chapel Hill, N.C., 1939), pp. 40–41; C. R. Boxer, *The Golden Age of Brazil, 1695–1750* (Berkeley, Cal., 1962) devotes a chapter and additional space to a splendid discussion.
[13] "The South American States," *DBR*, VI (July 1848), 14.
[14] *Cf* Fletcher M. Green's articles on gold mining in Georgia, North Carolina, and Virginia: *GHQ*, XIX (June 1935), 93–111 and (Sept. 1935), 210–28; *NCHR*, XIV (Jan. 1937), 1–19 and (Oct. 1937), 357–66. Significantly, the Southeastern developments were discussed in relation to California. See *DBR*, XVIII (Feb. 1855), 241–50.
[15] See, *e.g.*, Francis Terry Leak Diary, July 7, 1855.
[16] *DBR*, XXVIII (March 1860), 281.
[17] *Congressional Globe*, XIX, Part 2, 31st Congress, 1st Session, HR, Sept. 7, 1850.

[18] "The Irrepressible Conflict and the Impending Crisis," *DBR*, XXVIII (May 1860), 535.
[19] Clingman, *Speeches*, p. 239 (Jan. 22, 1850).
[20] *Speeches, Messages, and Other Writings* (ed. M. W. Cluskey; Philadelphia, 1859), p. 181.
[21] Delilah L. Beasley, "Slavery in California," *JNH*, III (Jan. 1918), 40–41.
[22] "Public Lands of Texas," *DBR*, XIII (July 1852), 54.
[23] Quoted in W. H. Watford, "Confederate Western Ambitions," *SHQ*, XLIV (Oct. 1940), 168.
[24] Brown, *Speeches, Messages*, p. 595; speech at Hazlehurst, Miss., Sept. 11, 1858.

mented the political barriers to the expansion of slavery into New Mexico's; it is another for us to conclude that their hopes and desires were more than wishful thinking. Allan Nevins has presented a formidable case to suggest that slavery had little room even in the mining districts of the Southwest and Mexico. He shows that even in the Gadsden Purchase the economic exigencies of mining brought about the quick suppression of the enterprising individual by the corporation. Western mining, as well as transportation, lumbering, and some forms of agriculture, required much capital and became fields for big business. High labor costs led to a rising demand for labor-saving machinery, but Nevins does not consider that this very condition might, under certain circumstances, have spurred the introduction of slave labor.[33] He writes:

For three salient facts stood out in any survey of the Far West. First, this land of plain and peak was natural soil for a free-spirited and highly competitive society, demanding of every resident skill and intelligence. It was, therefore, even in that Gadsden Purchase country which had been bought at the behest of the slave states, a country naturally inhospitable to slavery. Second, when so much energy was steadily flowing into western expansion, and such wide outlets for more effort existed there, it was impossible to think of the country turning to Caribbean areas for a heavy thrust southward. Its main forces moved naturally toward the sunset, where rich opportunities were hardly yet sampled. The cotton kingdom, which realized that the West gave little scope for its peculiar culture, might plan grandiose Latin American adventures; but it would get little support from other regions. And in the third place, conditions in the West demanded capital and organization on a broad scale; if it was a land for individualists, it was even more a land for corporate enterprise—a land for the businessman. Those who pondered these three facts could see that they held an ominous meaning for the South. The nearer Northwest had already done much to upset the old sectional balance, and the Far West, as it filled up, would do still more.[34]

On economic grounds Nevins' analysis has much to offer, but his remarks on the competitive struggle in the Southwest and on the inability of Southerners to get national support for Caribbean adventures do not prove nearly so much as he thinks. At most, they suggest that the North was strong enough to block slavery expansionism into the Southwest and frustrate Southern ambitions elsewhere. If so, the case for secession, from the proslavery viewpoint, was unanswerable.

Nevins' remarks illustrate the wisdom of other Southern arguments—that the South had to secure new land politically, not by economic advance, and that the South had to have guarantees of positive federal protection for slavery in the territories.[35] The *Charleston Mercury*, climaxing a decade of Southern complaints, insisted in 1860 that slavery would have triumphed in California's gold mining areas if Southerners had had assurances of protection for their property. . . .

The Southern demand for federal guarantees made sense, but even that did not go far enough. Ultimately, the South needed not equal protection for slave property but complete political control. If a given territory could be organized by a proslavery party, then slaveholders would feel free to migrate. Time would be needed to allow the slave population to catch up; meanwhile, free-soil farmers had to be kept out in favor of men who looked forward to becoming slaveholders. Under such circumstances the territory's population might grow very slowly, and the exploitation of its resources might lag far behind that of the free territories. Nothing essential would be lost to the South by underdevelopment; the South as a whole was underdeveloped. In short, the question of political power necessarily had priority over the strictly economic questions. . . .

For the moment let us consider Kansas as solely and inevitably a wheat

---

[33] *The Emergence of Lincoln* (2 vols.; New York, 1950), I, 330–31.
[34] *Ibid.*, I, 342.

[35] I find it strange that Nevins attacks this late antebellum demand as an abstraction; his own evidence indicates that it was of central importance to the slavery cause.

state. Large slave plantations have not proved well adapted to wheat growing, but small plantations were doing well in the Virginia tidewater. In open competition with Northwestern farmers the slaveholders probably would have been hurt badly. They knew as much. When, for example, Percy Roberts of Mississippi maintained that Negro slavery could thrive in the Northwest grain belt, he simultaneously maintained that the African slave trade would have to be re-opened to drive down the cost of labor and put the slaveholders in a favorable competitive position.[43] Historians like Nevins and Paul W. Gates have expressed confidence that slavery could not have triumphed in Kansas even if it had been allowed a foothold. They may be right, but only if one assumes that the South remained in the Union. Slavery expansionism required fastening proslavery regimes in such territories, but ultimately it required secession to protect the gains. Had Kansas joined a Southern Confederacy as a slave state, its wheat-growing slaveholders could have secured the same internal advantages as the sugar planters of Louisiana, and Union wheat could effectively have been placed at a competitive disadvantage in the Southern market.

Ramsdell's dismissal of Southern interest in Cuba and Central America, however necessary for his argument, does not bear examination. Southern sugar planters, who might have been expected to fear the glutting of the sugar market should Cuba enter the Union, spoke out for annexation. They seem to have been convinced that suspension of the African slave trade to Cuba would raise the cost of production there to American levels and that they would be able to buy Cuban slaves cheaply.[44] Besides, as Basil Rauch points out, Louisiana sugar planters were moving to Cuba during the 1850s and looking forward to extending their fortunes.[45] . . .

Opposition to territorial expansion by many Southerners has led some historians to deny the existence of an "aggressive slaveocracy" or to assert, with Ramsdell, that Southerners were too individualistic to be mobilized for such political adventures, which were often contrary to their private interests. No conspiracy theory is required. That there were many Southern leaders who sensed the need for more territory and fought for it is indisputable. That individual Southerners were not always willing to move when the interests of their class and system required them to merely indicates one of the ways in which slavery expansionism proved a contradictory process. Southerners opposed expansion for a variety of reasons, but mostly because they feared more free states. Expansion southward had the great advantage of not being cotton expansion, and the economic argument against it was weak. On the other hand, many feared that the annexation of Cuba would provide an excuse for the annexation of Canada or that the annexation of Mexico would repeat the experience of California. This opposition should be understood essentially as a preference for delaying expansion until secession had been effected, although there were, of course, many who opposed both.[50]

THE ANGUISH OF CONTRADICTION

If the slave South had to expand to survive, it paradoxically could not do so when given the opportunity. Unsettled political conditions prevented the immigration of slave property, much as the threat of nationalization or of a left-wing or nationalist coup prevents the flow of American capital to some underdeveloped countries to which it is invited.

[43] "African Slavery Adapted to the North and Northwest," *DBR*, XXV (Oct. 1858), 379–85.
[44] J. S. Thrasher, "Cuba and the United States," *DBR*, XVII (July 1854), 43–49.
[45] *American Interest in Cuba, 1848–1855* (New York, 1948), p. 200; James Stirling, *Letters from the Slave States* (London, 1857), pp. 127 ff; John S. C. Abbott, *South and North; or Impressions Received during a Trip to Cuba* (New York, 1860), pp. 52, 53. Texans, too, wanted Cuba. See Earl W. Fornell, "Agitation in Texas for Reopening the Slave Trade," *SHQ*, LX (Oct. 1956), 245–59.
[50] *SQR*, XXI (Jan. 1852), 3; see the arguments advanced by William Walker for avoiding an attempt to link Nicaragua with the Union, *The War in Nicaragua*, Chap. VIII.

"Where," asks Allan Nevins when discussing Kansas, "were proslavery settlers to come from? Arkansas, Texas, and New Mexico were all calling for slaveholding immigrants, and the two first were more attractive to Southerners than Kansas."[51] Slave property necessarily moved cautiously and slowly. So long as it had to move at the pace set by Northern farmers, it would be defeated. The mere fact of competition discouraged the movement of slaveholders, and if they were willing to move, they could not hope to carry enough whites to win.

An area could be safely absorbed by the slave regime only by preventing Northern free-soilers from entering. Danhof has demonstrated that farm making was an expensive business.[52] Northern farmers had a hard time; Southern farmers, without slaves or minimal savings, found it much harder. Traditionally, the more energetic nonslaveholders moved into new land first and cleared it; the planters followed much later.[53] If those early settlers had to secure the territory against free-soilism before the planters and slaveholders moved in, the struggle could not ordinarily be won. Many Southern nonslaveholders could be and were converted to the antislavery banner once they found themselves away from the power and influence of the slaveholders. . . . Their allegiance to the system rested ultimately on the ability of the slaveholders to retain political power and social and ideological leadership and to prevent these men of the lower classes from seeing an alternative way of life. Yet, by

1860 even Missouri had become a battleground because of its special geographic position and Northern and foreign immigration. Kansas could never be secured for slavery unless the slaveholders had political control and the migrating Southern farmers were isolated from corrupting influences. . . . Only if a territory shut out free-soil immigration, quickly established the political hegemony of the slaveholders, and prepared for a much slower development than Northerners might give it, could it be secured for slavery. These conditions negated slavery expansionism, but only so long as the South remained in the Union.

INVITATION TO A (SELF-INFLICTED) BEHEADING

The South had to expand, and its leaders knew it. "There is not a slaveholder in this House or out of it," Judge Warner of Georgia declared in the House of Representatives in 1856, "but who knows perfectly well that whenever slavery is confined within certain specified limits, its future existence is doomed."[57] The Republican party, said an editorial in *The Plantation* in 1860, denies that it wants to war on slavery, but it admits that it wants to surround it with free states. To do so would be to crush slavery where it now exists.[58] Percy L. Rainwater's study of sentiment in Mississippi in the 1850s shows how firmly convinced slaveholders were that the system had to expand or die.[59] . . . The extinction of slavery would have broken the power of the slaveholders in general and the planters in particular. Ideologically, these men had committed themselves to slaveholding and the plantation regime as the proper foundations of civilization. Politically, the preservation of their power depended on the preservation of its economic base. Economically, the plantation system would have tottered under free labor conditions and would have existed under some inter-

---

[51] *Ordeal of the Union*, II, 304.
[52] Clarence H. Danhof, "Farm-making Costs and the 'Safety Valve,' " *JPE*, XLIX (June 1941), 317–59. *Cf.* Nevins, *Emergence of Lincoln*, I, 159, on Kansas in the 1850s. Thomas Le Duc has argued that many farmers could and did squat in squalor while slowly building a farm: "Public Policy, Private Investment and Land Use in American Agriculture, 1825–1875," *Agr. Hist.*, XXXVII (Jan. 1963), 3–9. Even with this qualification, capital and resources were a big factor, and the competitive advantage of Northern farmers over Southern is beyond doubt. Only when circumstances permitted the massive movement of planters and slaves could the result be different.
[53] Yarbrough, *Economic Aspects of Slavery*, p. 104.

[57] Quoted in George M. Weston, *The Progress of Slavery in the United States* (Washington, D.C., 1857), p. 227.
[58] *The Plantation* (March 1860), pp. 1–2.
[59] "Economic Benefits of Secession: Opinions in Mississippi in the 1850's," *JSH*, I (Nov. 1935), 459 and *passim*.

mediary form like sharecropping only at the expense of the old ruling class. . . . The slaveholders knew their own power and could not help being suspicious of sweeping changes in their way of life, no matter how persuasively advanced. Their slaveholding psychology, habit of command, race pride, rural lordship, aristocratic pretensions, political domination, and economic strength militated in defense of the status quo. Under such circumstances an occasional voice warning that a conversion to tenantry or sharecropping carried serious dangers to their material interests sufficed to stiffen their resistance. . . .

Those who, like Max Weber, Ramsdell, even Phillips, and countless others, assume that the South could have accepted a peaceful transition to free labor gravely misjudge the character of its ruling class. . . .

The slaveholders, not the South, held the power to accede or resist. To these men slaves were a source of power, pride, and prestige, a duty and a responsibility, a privilege and a trust; slavery was the foundation of a special civilization imprinted with their own character. The defense of slavery, to them, meant the defense of their honor and dignity, which they saw as the essence of life. They could never agree to renounce the foundation of their power and moral sensibility and to undergo a metamorphosis into a class the nature and values of which were an inversion of their own. Slavery represented the cornerstone of their way of life, and life to them meant an honor and dignity associated with the power of command. When the slaveholders rose in insurrection, they knew what they were about: in the fullest sense, they were fighting for their lives.

SUGGESTIONS FOR ADDITIONAL READING

Further study should begin with the complete works from which the selections were drawn: David B. Davis, *The Problem of Slavery in Western Culture* (Ithaca, N.Y., 1966); Stanley Elkins, *Slavery* (Chicago, 1968);* Eugene D. Genovese, *The Political Economy of Slavery* (New York, 1967);* Marvin Harris, *Patterns of Race in the Americas* (New York, 1964); Harmannus Hoetink, *The Two Variants in Caribbean Race Relations* (New York, 1967); Winthrop D. Jordan, *White Over Black* (Chapel Hill, N.C., 1968); Herbert S. Klein, *Slavery in the Americas: A Comparative Study of Virginia and Cuba* (Chicago, 1967); Leon F. Litwack, *North of Slavery* (Chicago, 1961);* Kenneth M. Stampp, *The Peculiar Institution* (New York, 1956);* Frank Tannenbaum, *Slave and Citizen* (New York, 1946);* Thad W. Tate, *The Negro in Eighteenth-Century Williamsburg* (Williamsburg, 1964).* The footnotes in these works will introduce the rich variety of primary and secondary sources which exist in print. Moreover Genovese, Jordan, and Litwack provide annotated bibliographies which serve as guides to the topics they discuss.

General works treating slavery as an integral part of American culture are scarce, so students seeking a general view must begin with books which concentrate on slavery and the Negro. John Hope Franklin, *From Slavery to Freedom,* 3rd ed. (New York, 1967) is a standard textbook of Negro history and contains an extensive annotated bibliography. Useful general collections of primary documents may be found in Herbert Aptheker, *Documentary History of the Negro People in the United States* (New York, 1951); and Leslie H. Fishel and Benjamin Quarles, *The Negro American: A Documentary History* (Glenview, Ill., 1967).* W. E. B. DuBois, *Black Folk, Then and Now: An Essay in the History and Sociology of the Negro Race* (New York, 1939) expresses important insights from an unconventional perspective.

Students wishing to explore particular questions raised by the readings can turn to an extensive body of special studies dealing with a wide variety of topics. There are so many works that the following references are just a sample and can only suggest the wealth of scholarship available. The context of attitudes and ideas in which American slavery developed is thoroughly and imaginatively explored in Winthrop D. Jordan, *White Over Black: The Development of American Attitudes Toward the Negro, 1550–1812* (Chapel Hill, N.C., 1968);* and William R. Stanton, *The Leopard's Spots: Scientific Attitudes toward Race in America, 1815–1859* (Chicago, 1960).* Jordan's work also includes a critical bibliography. Black attitudes are revealed in Carter G. Woodson, *The Mind of the Negro as Reflected in Letters Written During the Crisis, 1800–1860* (Washington, D.C., 1926); and James M. McPherson, *The Negro's Civil War* (New York, 1965).* The development of slavery and race relations in a variety of regional and temporal settings may be viewed in James C. Ballagh, *A History of Slavery in Virginia* (Baltimore, 1902); Frank J. Klingberg, *An Appraisal of the Negro in Colonial South Carolina* (Washington, D.C., 1941); Charles S. Sydnor, *Slavery in Mississippi* (New York, 1933);* James B. Sellers, *Slavery in Alabama* (University, Ala., 1950); Chase C. Mooney, *Slavery in Tennessee* (Bloomington, Ind., 1957); Edward R. Turner, *The Negro in Pennsylvania* (Washington, D.C., 1911); Lorenzo J. Greene, *The Negro in Colonial New England* (New York, 1942);* Arthur Zilversmit, *The First Emancipation: The Abolition of Slavery in the North* (Chicago, 1967). Classic general interpretations of the South are presented in Ulrich B. Phillips, *American Negro Slavery* (New York, 1918)* and his *Life and Labor in the Old South* (Boston, 1929).* They should be read in conjunction with Richard Hofstadter's critique, "U. B. Phillips

* available in paperback

107

and the Plantation Legend," *Journal of Negro History*, XXIX (April, 1944). Kenneth M. Stampp's *The Peculiar Institution* (New York, 1956)* provides a general view of slavery as seen by a northern liberal. A brilliant contemporary portrait is Frederick Law Olmsted, *The Cotton Kingdom* (New York, 1861). For purposes of comparison historians have found Gilberto Freyre, *The Masters and the Slaves: A Study in the Development of Brazilian Civilization* (New York, 1946) particularly interesting.

The interaction between slavery and urban life is examined in Richard C. Wade, *Slavery in the Cities: The South, 1820–1860* (New York, 1964). One of the most significant works on slavery as an economic system is Alfred H. Conrad and John R. Meyer, *The Economics of Slavery and other Econometric Studies* (Chicago, 1964). Students should also consult Harold D. Woodman, *Slavery and the Southern Economy: Sources and Readings* (New York, 1966).* The slave trade itself is ably described in Daniel P. Mannix, *Black Cargoes: A History of the Atlantic Slave Trade, 1518–1865* (New York, 1962). Relations between free and slave labor are presented in John Spencer Bassett, *Slavery and Servitude in the Colony of North Carolina* (Baltimore, 1896); Marcus W. Jernegan, *Laboring and Dependent Classes in Colonial America, 1607–1783* (Chicago, 1931); and Richard B. Morris, *Government and Labor in Early America* (New York, 1946).* Key aspects of social relations among Americans in the slave South are treated in Avery O. Craven, "Poor Whites and Negroes in the Antebellum South," *Journal of Negro History*, XV (January, 1930); and James H. Johnston, *Miscegenation in the Ante-Bellum South* (Chicago, 1939). Herbert Aptheker, *American Negro Slave Revolts* (New York, 1943)* explores another crucial area of social relations. Race relations in time of war are presented in Benjamin Quarles, *The Negro in the American Revolution* (Chapel Hill, N.C., 1961) and his *The Negro in the Civil War* (Boston, 1953); as well as in James M. McPherson, *The Struggle for Equality: Abolitionists and the Negro in Civil War and Reconstruction* (Princeton, 1964). The best introductory anthology is Allen Weinstein and Frank O. Gatell, eds., *American Negro Slavery* (New York, 1968).*

The body of literature treating antislavery is immense, but Louis Filler, *The Crusade Against Slavery, 1830–1860* (New York, 1960),* provides an excellent introduction and offers an authoritative annotated bibliography.

45678910